ENDORSEMENTS

"We are living in a time that demands not just more leadership, but a new kind of leadership—one that is wise, whole, inclusive, and deeply human. Amy Powell's *Rise Like a Woman* is a beautifully written, fiercely honest, and powerfully practical guide to cultivating that leadership from the inside out. It is a clarion call to women everywhere to stop waiting, stop shrinking, and rise fully into their strength, purpose, and presence.

"As the co-founder of Conscious Capitalism and co-author of *Shakti Leadership*, I have long believed that the future of business—and the healing of our world—depends on the full flourishing of women in leadership. This book offers not just inspiration, but a roadmap. Amy draws from her own hard-won experience and decades of coaching and consulting to illuminate seven powerful strategies that help women rise not despite who they are, but because of who they are.

"In these pages, you will find wisdom born of courage, tools forged in the fire of adversity, and stories that will stir your soul. You will also find something rare and precious: the belief that your rising matters—not just for you, but for all of us.

"We need more women at the highest levels of leadership—not someday, but now. *Rise Like a Woman* shows us why and, more importantly, shows us how."

—**Raj Sisodia,** Co-Founder of Conscious Capitalism
Co-Author of *Shakti Leadership*

"Rise Like a Woman is an insightful and empowering guide for mid-career women navigating professional crossroads. Drawing on years of experience working with global leaders, Amy has more recently supported highly qualified (and often underemployed) international women to build confidence and gain tools to advance their careers.

"This book is a grounded, compassionate roadmap for anyone seeking meaningful growth without compromising their values."

—Suzanne Sierra,
Executive Director, St. Louis Mosaic Project

"Amy Powell doesn't just coach women, she transforms how they see themselves and their potential, and this book, *Rise Like a Woman,* beautifully encapsulates Amy's wisdom and experience.

"Over a decade ago, when I was navigating the challenging path from middle management to senior management, Amy encouraged me to go the distance rather than settle for safety and invisibility. Her insights and coaching helped me understand that reaching the C-Suite level wasn't just about personal advancement; it was about gaining influence to help reshape organisational cultures and create workplaces where everyone can thrive, not just your stereotypical 'masculine' leader.

"This book captures Amy's rare ability to see potential where others see obstacles, and her seven strategies are both practical and profound. Every woman who aspires to senior leadership or knows deep down they have the talent but wonders if it's worth it due to the challenges and constraints they see in their current workplace—and every organisation that wants to unlock the full potential of their female talent—needs this roadmap. Amy doesn't just help women rise; she helps them rise in a way that lifts everyone around them."

—Deanne Stewart, CEO, Aware Super

"With deep insight gained from years of coaching hundreds of professionals—women and men at every career stage and across a wide range of industries and cultural backgrounds—Amy Powell's *Rise Like a Woman: 7 Strategies to Step Up, Stand Out, and Succeed at Work* is a practical, empowering guide for anyone seeking greater fulfillment in their professional life.

"Far more than a collection of career tips, this book is a research-informed roadmap designed to help readers align their values and unique strengths with actionable, results-driven strategies. Challenging the limiting assumptions that too often hold women back, the author shows how moving beyond career impasses and stepping into higher-impact roles can lead not only to greater influence but also to more freedom and satisfaction at work.

"Weaving in honest, relatable stories drawn from her life and from the journeys of her clients, Amy Powell brings these strategies to life, offering both inspiration and practical direction. Whether you're just starting out, navigating a turning point, or seeking fresh momentum as a seasoned professional, *Rise Like a Woman* meets you where you are—and will help you move forward with clarity, confidence, and purpose."

—Barbara L. Gross, PhD
Professor Emerita of Marketing
California State University, Northridge

"Many of the women in the Westpac Foundation & Scholars Trust, me included, have had the privilege of participating in Amy's program—and it's made a real and lasting impact. From building confidence to learning practical strategies for career development and leadership, the tools we gained have helped us grow not only as professionals but also as people.

"I'm thrilled that Amy has captured this powerful content in a book, making it accessible to any woman ready to take charge of her development and thrive at work. These are actionable, real-world strategies—and they work."

—Amy Lyden, CEO,
The Westpac Foundation & Scholars Trust

"What Amy Powell has captured in *Rise Like a Woman* reflects exactly what I've seen her do in practice: she meets women where they are and helps them translate the unfamiliar into something accessible, empowering, and actionable. Her seven strategies aren't just theoretical; they are deeply human, brilliantly practical, and rooted in a genuine desire to help women rise in alignment with who they are, not who they're expected to be.

"This book speaks not only to individual growth but also to something larger: the transformation of workplace culture and the redefinition of what leadership can—and should— look like.

"Amy doesn't just show us how to rise, she shows us why we must. Because, as she writes, we need more women at the top. Not just for equity, but because when women rise, everyone rises—organizations, communities, families, and futures.

"If you're a woman who's ever wondered whether leadership is worth it, or if it's even possible to succeed without losing yourself, *Rise like a Woman* has the answer. It's your companion, your coach, and your call to action."

—Susan Gobbo, Co-Founder/Program Director, International Mentoring St Louis (IMSTL)

"In *Rise Like a Woman*, Amy Powell offers practical, empowering tools to help women at every stage of their careers rise and make a meaningful impact in the workplace. Having had the privilege of working with Amy in various contexts, I'm delighted to see her wisdom, support, and guidance now available to a wider audience through this book.

"Rich with insights, this is a book to read slowly—savoring each chapter, reflecting on its lessons, and experimenting with the methods to see what works best for you. *Rise Like a Woman* invites us to transform not only how we work but also how we experience our work."

—Wojtyla Kmiecik Moreira, Plant Manager, ICL Group

"In *Rise Like a Woman*, Amy Powell delivers a compelling roadmap for women navigating the complexities of the workplace. Combining research, real-life examples, and practical exercises, Powell equips readers with essential tools to rise through their strengths, build meaningful connections, and find purpose in their work. This book is an inspiring call to action for women to claim their space at the top and lead with confidence and compassion."

—C.J. Hayden, Author, *Overcoming the Fear of Self-Promotion*

"Amy Powell has applied decades of experience as an executive coach into this practical, engaging book full of personal insights, shared stories, and lessons to create a must-read guide for women aspiring to leadership.

"The book also contains equally valuable context and perspectives for male leaders who aspire to support women in their career growth. Understanding the inherent biases, structures, and challenges is essential for any leader who wants to enable others to reach their potential and make a difference at work."

—**Matthew Rady,** CEO, BT Financial

"Reflection, courage, honesty, and insight—Amy Powell brings these essential leadership qualities to life in *Rise Like a Woman*. She shines a light on the roadblocks that can hold us back—fear of failure, the need to be perfect before considering opportunities, that relentless inner critic questioning our right to lead—and offers practical strategies to overcome them. Amy's wisdom, drawn from her journey and the exceptional women she has coached, is a treasure trove for anyone ready to grow in confidence, self-awareness, and impact.

"Women have the capacity to lead in extraordinary ways—balancing many demands and doing so with skill and grace. Amy helps us see that potential clearly and claim it fully. As a global leader in culture transformation, purpose, and performance, she leads with authenticity and courage, walking her talk and inspiring others to do the same. Her determined and conscious support of women has transformed many careers, mine included, and her counsel is as wise as it is empowering."

—**Robyn Whittaker,** Chief People Officer
Norton Rose Fulbright – Australian Region

"The most meaningful and impactful self-help books are those that are based on real-life transformations, insights based on long-term experience, and practical and smart suggestions. Amy Powell's *Rise Like a Woman* contains all three. If you are a woman who wants to lead an authentic, fulfilled, and successful life, then this is for you."

—**Joan Shafer,** Executive Mentor, The Exco Group
Co-Founder of the Barrett Values Centre

"Rise Like a Woman should be read by all—and all men. Amy Powell has a rare gift for unlocking and empowering women without trying to change them.

"Her book celebrates the truth that the magic of women lies in being unapologetically themselves. Amy's magic inspires us all to become better humans."

—**Tony Bulmer,** Founder and CEO
Bulmer Group International

RISE
LIKE A
WOMAN

7 Strategies to Step Up, Stand Out,
and Succeed at Work

AMY POWELL

Stonebrook Publishing
Saint Louis, Missouri

A STONEBROOK PUBLISHING BOOK
©2025 Amy Powell
This book was guided in development and
edited by Nancy L. Erickson, The Book Professor®
TheBookProfessor.com

Library of Congress Control Number: 2025912553

Paperback ISBN: 978-1-955711-40-1
eBook ISBN: 978-1-955711-41-8

www.stonebrookpublishing.net
PRINTED IN THE UNITED STATES OF AMERICA

"I can promise you that women working together
—linked, informed, and educated—
can bring peace and prosperity to this forsaken planet."

—Isabel Allende

CONTENTS

INTRODUCTION: WOMEN AND WORK

DID YOU PICK up this book because you're a working woman who wants to get "unstuck" and move up in your organization? And—if possible—you'd like to do it in a way that aligns with your strengths and values, while not requiring you to sell your soul? Well, hang on. This book will help you do those things, but there's more to it than that.

I wrote *Rise Like a Woman* for two reasons. The first one is obvious: to meet your needs, which I care deeply about. I've worked with hundreds of women like you, and I feel as if I know you. I want you to have a career where you can grow and advance in a way that's authentic to you, one that utilizes the strengths you bring to the workplace, and that brings you fulfillment. Most of this book focuses on how to achieve that.

The second reason is more subtle and even a bit subversive. I wrote this book to encourage you and your female colleagues to go the distance because we need strong women leading at the highest levels in corporations and organizations.

We need women like you to make organizations more successful and at the same time make businesses more human. We need your untethered talent. We need the breadth of your perspective.

We need you to make business the best it can be—the best for other women at every stage in their lives; the best for men who also want to be fully engaged in both life and work, and the best for children, who benefit when their parents thrive.

We need you to create a bridge between organizations and the communities they are part of, as we are emboldened to bring values of compassion and fairness and kindness to the workplace.

We need you to create a path forward for the planet and the future, as we remind ourselves that we are now imagining and designing the world our families will inherit.

We need women at the top. And there's something wrong because, to a large extent, they still aren't there.

According to 2023 research from Standard and Poor's (S&P), women in publicly traded companies now make up less than 12 percent of the C-Suite, whereas they represent 47 percent of the overall workforce. That means they don't have the same influence, power, or salaries as their male counterparts. The world of the C-Suite is clearly still dominated by men, and women who do reach this level are still considered anomalies. As of the time this book is written, there is no sign that the situation is improving. In fact, we seem to be going the opposite direction.

> **WE NEED WOMEN AT THE TOP. AND THERE'S SOMETHING WRONG BECAUSE, TO A LARGE EXTENT, THEY STILL AREN'T THERE.**

We can't fall back on the old response that progress will happen naturally and we only need to give it time. Women entered the US workforce en masse in the 1960s through the 1980s. We've had two generations to get to parity at those senior levels. But we aren't there. And businesses, though they may not realize it, are paying a price for that. There is a growing body of research that shows that organizations with women in the C-Suite and on boards are more successful than their counterparts who don't have women at those levels. For example:

1. McKinsey and Company has conducted a series of studies, finding that companies in the top quartile for gender diversity on executive teams were 25 percent more likely to have above-average profitability compared to those companies in the bottom quartile. They also showed that there are correlations between gender diversity in leadership and higher financial performance, advances through innovation, and employee retention.

2. S&P Global released a report that showed that organizations with female CEOs or CFOs had stronger stock price performance and profit margins in the two years following their appointments, and specifically, those with female CEOs delivered 34 percent better profit growth and 8 percent better stock returns while they were in the role.

3. The Credit Suisse Research Institute pointed out that companies with at least one woman on the board had better share price performance and higher returns on equity than those that had no women on their board.

We have repeatedly seen that women aren't rising through the ranks as we would expect them to. We know about the "broken rung" that occurs early in their step up to leadership, but I've seen another break that comes later in careers. That break happens when mid-level and senior women realize the workplace isn't meeting their needs or expectations. If women aren't blocked by the systemic discrimination they often experience, they're sometimes stepping out because they don't like what they see. They aren't sure that the price of reaching senior management is worth the tradeoffs in a world where senior management expectations are often designed for a traditionally male way of life.

> IF YOU KEEP ADVANCING TO MORE SENIOR LEVELS, YOUR JOB PROBABLY WON'T BE HARDER OR MORE LIMITING. YOU'LL HAVE A TEAM OF SMART PEOPLE WORKING FOR YOU AND SUPPORTING YOU.

There's a very understandable hesitation women experience once they've stepped into their first or second management role. Women often ask (quietly), "Do I really want the hassle of senior leadership? My job is hard enough. I want to be there for my family. I want to spend quality time with my children while they are growing up." As I talk to women who've been selected for high-potential women's programs, some doubt that it's worth it to move up. Many prefer to sit in mid-level roles (for mid-level incomes) rather than aspire to the most senior levels. They think they'll lose the freedom to be a whole person.

But I have news for you. If you keep advancing to more senior levels, your job probably won't be harder or more limiting. You'll have a team of smart people working for you and supporting you. And you won't lose your freedom. You will be, in many ways, freer. You'll be able to make decisions that will help other women (and men) be whole people.

You may find that hard to believe. Here's why I'm saying this: I've interviewed hundreds of mid-level and senior-level leaders, and it's the mid-level leaders who are struggling. A big part of my consulting career has been spent conducting organizational culture surveys for companies. One thing we found in our surveys was this: in many organizations (and in all those I worked with), middle managers had the hardest jobs of anyone in the organizational hierarchy. They're the most frustrated, and they rate their experience more negatively than the people who work below them or above them. Repeatedly, they say that they feel like the "meat in the sandwich." They feel the pressure, the expectations, and the needs of the people who work for them. At the same time, they're limited in their budgets and resources and are constantly expected to do more with less.

CONSEQUENTLY, PAUSING YOUR CAREER INDEFINITELY AT MIDDLE MANAGEMENT LEVELS IS UNLIKELY TO RESULT IN A HAPPIER CAREER.

Unsurprisingly, the satisfaction of middle managers is lower. However, when they move up in the hierarchy, something unexpected happens. As they move from middle levels to senior levels, their engagement goes up, and their sense of satisfaction and fulfillment rises. Why? Because they can be strategic, they can make informed decisions, and they have good people below them who will execute and drive results. Consequently, pausing your career indefinitely at middle management levels is unlikely to result in a happier career.

In addition, business has been built using a model that helped men thrive, not women.

In Caroline Criado Perez's book *Invisible Women: Data Bias in a World Designed for Men,* she showed dozens of examples that decried the false assumption that "what's good for men is good for all." The most famous example was the use of crash test dummies designed to create safety features that fit the average man. This resulted in women being 47 percent more likely to be seriously injured in a car accident, 71 percent more likely to be moderately injured, and 17 percent more likely to die.

How many ways has business been designed to meet the needs of men who have stay-at-home wives? One example is that the length and hours of the standard work week are not aligned with the length and hours of school days. This fact is rarely questioned or taken seriously as a genuine systemic enabler for the advantage of men with stay-at-home partners to move up without impediment.

However, it doesn't have to remain that way. I'm here to encourage you that it's worth staying the course. The workplace needs women who will disrupt the status quo to make this a more woman-friendly (and human-friendly) world. And to change things in almost all organizations, you must make it to the top. I hope that these ideas will help you work more effectively to get there, and I hope to convince you that it's worth going through occasional turbulence along the way.

Tara Mohr, in her paradigm-shifting book *Playing Big,* says, "If we want to make a distinctive impact on our communities or organizations and make positive change, we need a different set of skills. We need to effectively *challenge authority*, not just adapt to it. We need to *influence* authority figures, not just please them."

For most of history, women have only been able to persuade from behind a metaphorical curtain. They've tried to be the invisible conscience that influences their men: husbands, brothers, and fathers. And they did it without the education, without the vote, without formal power, without the ability to work in more than a handful of professions. But it's time to step firmly into the world of business, to bring women's values and needs into play, and to ultimately change the way we work.

My goal now, for the rest of this book, is to support you in finding work where you excel, work that makes a difference, and work that brings you joy.

So, what do *you* want?

MAKING YOUR CAREER WORK FOR YOU

One of the first questions I ask coaching clients at the start of their coaching journey is deceptively simple: "What do you really want from your work and career?" It's a practical question from my perspective. If our coaching is to be successful, I need to know the answer. I don't want to link arms and skip down the yellow-brick road that's in my head. I need to know what's in your head and your heart.

Women, in particular, can be stumped by this question. I often ask it in a room of women, which can be a powerful "aha" experience, because they think, *It's not just me. A lot of people don't know the answer to this question.*

Why don't women know the answer? I believe it's harder for women than men because they've been shaped by expectations from others that have left them confused and off-balance. They say, "I want. . .

- To be a leader, but I care deeply about people, and I'm afraid I might have to give that up to be in charge (e.g., my manager has already told me I need to be tougher with others)."
- A big leadership role, but I don't want to miss out on my child's first day of school or any of the other important childhood moments."
- A great promotion, but not if it means that I'll have to spend less time with my family or have to move them away from friends and relatives."

One other reason women struggle with this question is that we don't think we should ask for what we want. As dutiful employees, daughters, wives, and mothers, we often feel that our lives belong to everyone else. To ask for what we want has not been encouraged or, in extreme cases, even allowed. Some international women I've worked with have said that becoming a physician was the only career acceptable to their families and that there was no concern for their talents or interests. Talk about creating a high bar. As one high-achieving woman said: "My family feels that, as a banker, I have nothing useful to offer them and their friends."

Women from some Asian, European, and Central and South American cultures speak about the intense pressure of family-of-origin cultural expectations. Many are expected to provide financial and physical care for their parents, even if that means living in the same town, village, or on a farm for their entire lives. In Australia, women who come from working-class backgrounds are sometimes cautioned not to become "tall poppies"—don't stand out, or you'll get cut down. In the US and many other places, there's a long tradition of women being relegated to roles as teachers, nurses, or caregivers. Traditionally, these have been the only roles that allowed individuals to balance caring for their families.

However, it's not just these cultures. Women from every culture are being shaped by the limitations and expectations of their environments. Maybe there are cultures where women are urged to reach for the stars, but I didn't come from a background like that, nor do most of the women I work with.

And what's more, what we want at eighteen or twenty-two shouldn't shape our entire lives. Our needs and expectations can and will change many times. It's worth asking ourselves some questions, and trust me on this, you don't just ask them at one point in your life. Ask, *Am I on track? Do I feel good about my work?* for as long as you go to work every day. Our work (paid and unpaid) takes up most of our waking hours. Let's get it right.

HOW TO READ THIS BOOK

In the coming strategies, you'll learn seven ways to rise like a woman. From there, you'll find inspiration and practical strategies for success that may have eluded you in the past. By the end, my hope is that you'll embrace these ideas and grow into the leader you can become.

I encourage you to start at the beginning and work your way through to the end of the book. The strategies will build upon each other and come together at the end.

For example:

- You need to have clarity about your strengths. . .
- So you'll know what you want to stand for at work. . .
- And be able to make your strengths and purpose visible to others. . .
- Which will require some courageous conversations. . .
- That will help you find the connections you want. . .
- And the champions you need. . .
- So that you find, and do, the work that matters to you—work that you love.

Let's get started.

STRATEGY 1

RISE THROUGH YOUR STRENGTHS

"A strong woman understands that the gifts such as logic, decisiveness, and strength are just as feminine as intuition and emotional connection. She values and uses all of her gifts."

—Nancy Rathburn

CLIMBING ABOARD THE corporate train, I had high hopes for my chosen career as an entry-level accountant. But within weeks, it became obvious that this journey wasn't going where I thought it would. Hard work, my can-do attitude, and good grades collided with my death-eater first boss (DEFB).

However, before I take you to the scene of the disaster, let me provide some background information. In my early twenties, I worked as an assistant manager at a retirement home by day and studied for an MBA at night. I excelled in all my classes and enjoyed the challenges of finance and accounting, subjects that weren't easy for me. I worked hard, got straight As, and learned to see the world through a new lens.

Businesses would always need accountants, so I settled on finance as a career objective. It felt safe. Filled with confidence and optimism as my MBA neared completion, I felt ready to take on a hard-core business role and landed a job as a cost accountant at a large, respected corporation in defense contract work. But the grim reality of the actual role, at least in this company, knocked the wind out of me.

It was awful. There was no onboarding, no training, and no connecting the dots as to how the job fit in with anything else.

Invisible, beneath the notice of others, I sat at a secretary's desk (rather than with the other accountants) with a pile of paper reports I had to check for accuracy after I'd painstakingly entered data from another pile of paper reports. And I didn't have a clue what made these particular reports accurate or inaccurate. I slowly drowned, too terrified to ask for clarification. When I did, DEFB, a red-faced middle-aged man, blew his top and swore. "What did they $*%@ teach you in college?" Of course, he said this in front of my coworkers. When he stormed out of his office (he always stormed), my brain turned into overcooked oatmeal.

Determined to turn the situation around, I asked my colleagues for help, and I gradually began to understand the context and mechanics of the tasks. But even as I started to get the hang of it, DEFB wouldn't let it go: he barked orders, swore at me, and never bothered to hide his contempt.

After about four months of this, one of my coworkers stopped by my desk late one afternoon. "DEFB wants to see you now—in his office." He looked at me with the sympathetic eyes of someone who knew I was about to take a beating. The office was just around the corner, but the trip there felt like an eternity.

When I got there, I saw DEFB behind his large desk. A young woman I didn't know sat next to him. "This is Kim from Human Resources. We're going to let you go," he announced, emotionless. "But before you go, I want you to understand why. This is a spreadsheet I put together of what you've cost the business in the time you've been here. This all comes out of my budget. You don't contribute a single thing, and you *cost* me money." He pushed the incriminating spreadsheet across his desk for me to look at.

I stared at him and stammered, "But I've worked so hard to get better. I've gotten the reports in on time with no errors."

"Maybe so, but you'll never be an accountant. You're damned useless here. I'm leaving for the day. You stay here with Kim and do the paperwork."

In an instant, I knew it was true. I *was* damned useless. My last remaining flicker of self-worth evaporated.

Back then, self-help books hadn't yet created the phrase "impostor syndrome," but this was even worse. I'd been called out by my boss as an impostor—a fraud who pretended to be a cost accountant.

Kim showed me the paperwork I had to sign while the clock in the corner ticked. Neither of us seemed to know what to say. I cried the entire time, tears smudging my signatures.

To exit the building, I had to do the walk of shame past my coworkers. With puffy red eyes and a nose that had been running for an hour (of course, DEFB hadn't thought to provide tissues), my humiliation would be complete. Kim mercifully suggested that I stay in the office to wait for them to go. She shut the door as she left.

I sat there, numb. After a while, I heard the pop of latches on briefcases, the scrape of chair legs across the vinyl tiles, and waited until the low murmurs of conversation disappeared. They were gone. I peeked out, still red-eyed, and gathered my things and left. My stomach churned. When I got home, I threw up and went to bed.

After this, I couldn't find the courage to apply for another accounting job—or any job, for that matter. Humiliated and devastated, some mornings I couldn't get out of bed.

Gradually, I realized that DEFB had been half right. My strengths were not in the world of cost accounting. I could do the work if I had to. I could read financial statements and generate reports. But I had to work twice as hard as others to make it tell a story. I did not have the soul of an accountant.

As I talked to successful people and read every book I could find about careers, career paths, career setbacks, and career bellyflops, I realized that the career journey I had started was not right for me.

My strengths lay in other directions.

I cared about other people. My soul wanted to help them grow. So, I switched my career to human resources, where I went from strength to strength, continuing to learn and grow. Eventually becoming an external consultant, I ultimately moved on to create strong organizational cultures and finally ended up in executive coaching. I worked one-on-one with people who valued my expertise, often in the world of finance, sometimes several pay grades above DEFB. My work made me buzz with happiness. I'd found the work I was meant to do. And I haven't looked back.

THE PROBLEM WITH THE WAY WE USED TO VALUE STRENGTH

Women have been repressed and suppressed from the beginning of time for one core reason: they didn't have the physical strength of men. And here were some of the outcomes:

- Men could overpower women sexually, which made them even more vulnerable due to pregnancy and childbearing.
- In ancient times, countless women and girls were offered as human sacrifices to appease the gods.
- Societies often considered women to be their fathers' or their husbands' possessions. As a result, women didn't have the freedom or access to wealth that men had.
- Women, the (physically) weaker sex, weren't granted the right to education, so they lacked the means to participate in ideas and work that could improve their lot in life. Tragically, we still see this in some societies. Even today, girls who try to go to school in some cultures are beaten and enslaved—even raped and murdered.
- Until the twentieth century, women were denied the right to vote and, therefore, to influence their communities. Those who dared to protest were belittled, even abused and tortured.

Except for a few queens (and then, only in situations where there wasn't a qualified male heir) and very rare matriarchal societies, being a leader has not been an option for women. Throughout history, we have seen power go to the greatest military leaders. And those leaders were always men. From the Roman Empire right up to the twentieth century, Western cultures focused on physical strength to resolve differences and to gain power and leadership.

Even today, accepting women as leaders of men can be problematic. Because of the strength differential, there has been a longstanding conscious and unconscious assumption, often backed by divine decree, that women are simply not up to the job of leadership. This has been true in both Eastern and Western traditions.

"Times have changed," I hear you say. "We now see women in the C-Suite."

The reality? According to Standard and Poor's research, women in publicly traded companies lost C-Suite ground in 2023 for the first time since 2005. Women held only 11.8 percent of the approximately fifteen thousand C-Suite positions in publicly traded US firms, down from 12.2 percent in 2022.

The truth is that there's a global, unconscious belief that women aren't strong enough to lead. Men have carried this residual belief and passed it down through generations. And yes, even some women agree. As we know from body language studies, women have learned to stay small to avoid being a threat to others. And, as Adam Grant wrote in his 2023 *New York Times* essay, "Women Know Exactly What They are Doing When They Use 'Weak Language,'" many smart women have learned to be tentative in their communication.

Grant says that successful women intentionally sound some-what uncertain when they communicate, so they won't appear too strong and overpowering. This may seem counterintuitive, given that so many women have been told to be more asser-tive. And it may feel inauthentic to some. However, according to Grant's research, "weak language" helps women become more successful.

Through my work as an executive coach, I've seen the value that women bring to the leadership table. In the 1990s, every single one of my clients was a man. Few women were senior enough to merit their company's investment in lead-ership development. The men I coached had been taught to be leaders by old-style, competitive male managers, who often used their power to control, demand, and even demean the people who worked for and with them.

However, by the 1990s, sufficient research had emerged to make it clear that this approach wasn't working very well. Evidence-based research about leadership helped change the predominant paradigm of Theory X—the belief that people are motivated by desire for rewards and fear of punishment, that intimidation works, and that people need to be super-vised closely—to Theory Y—the belief that people want to do well, are motivated by appreciation, want to be involved in decisions, and like to have personal relationships at work. The managers I coached needed to learn new ways to lead and motivate others in a workplace that was very different from the one they had entered.

Take Alex as an example. A thirty-five-year-old insti-tutional banker, Alex had moved to a division of the bank he considered to be soft and "too nice" compared to the cutthroat, competitive division where he'd worked for the past ten years. After he'd butted heads with others in the new environment, he came to me, without much enthusiasm, for executive coaching. Over the next few sessions, it dawned on him that he hadn't gotten great results with his bulldozer approach. And he was even more surprised to learn what others thought of him through 360-degree feedback. They disliked his constant competitiveness and pressure.

This feedback, combined with solid research, helped Alex see that the way he was working wasn't actually working for him. He wasn't alone. Almost every male client I worked with then needed to change their behavior to get better results. They needed to:

- Curb their competitive desire to defeat their peers
- Get input from others prior to making decisions, rather than issuing decrees
- Share information that would be valuable to others rather than hoard it for their own benefit
- Listen to understand and gain perspective rather than respond and argue
- Show empathy and care in their communication rather than interrupting or speaking over others
- Give positive feedback when someone does something well rather than criticizing them for small imperfections

When they learned these new ways to lead (huge challenges for them, and I loved them for their persistence and hard work), they were nearly always measurably more effective as leaders than they'd been before. These skills repeatedly helped them improve team engagement, staff retention, and productivity.

At the end of our coaching engagement, Alex internalized this new way of working and returned to his original division with the confidence and commitment to take the new leadership approach with him. And it worked—even in the more competitive business environment. He brought a refreshing and effective way of leading.

Around ten years later, when women had grown into roles that were senior enough for their companies to invest in coaching for them, I observed a clear contrast to my all-male coaching clients. I thought the women would have consciously and unconsciously absorbed the aggressive behaviors of their male colleagues. While that was true for a few, for most of my female clients, those behaviors didn't show up. Most of them had a natural tendency to be collegiate. They solicited input from others, listened well, showed empathy and care, and gave positive feedback. They had other things they needed to work on (and we'll talk about some of those later in the book), but they brought powerful strengths as leaders.

Women often don't recognize their positive leadership qualities, so that's what we're going to talk about. Ask yourself, *What qualities do I bring as part of my personal package? What would I say if someone asked me what my strengths are?*

Let's find out.

WHAT ARE STRENGTHS, ANYWAY? The *Longman Dictionary of Contemporary English* describes a strength as "a particular quality or ability that gives someone or something an advantage." Based on this definition, a strength is anything that's inherently part of you that gives you an edge. This could be a natural talent, a well-developed skill, your IQ, your warm personality, or your integrity. The list could go on indefinitely.

Allow me to interject two important rules about strengths that are central to this book.

1. Whenever possible, adapt your work environment to your strengths, rather than the other way around.
2. If you don't enjoy it at least some of the time, it's not a strength. For our purposes, strengths are both those things you are good at and those you care about and enjoy.

Let's talk about these two rules.

ADAPT YOUR WORK ENVIRONMENT TO YOUR STRENGTHS

Your best work environment is one that uses your strengths. Most people approach life in the opposite way. They say to themselves, *This job requires me to be strong in areas that are weaknesses for me. I must do better.* And they work and work to overcome those weaknesses. This seems to make sense, but it takes very, very hard work to turn a weakness into a strength.

Some of the most miserable people I've seen are those who land a role that is simply not right for them, a role in which they have no opportunity to use their strengths. They think they must overcome this challenge through effort—and perhaps a personality graft.

Yes, you need to do the job well, and you need to tick those boxes. But you must also be in a position where you can share your strengths at work. Avoid roles where you spend your precious, finite energy overcoming your weaknesses. It's far better to use that energy to build on what you've got. To be successful and fulfilled at work, find a job where you have a shot at greatness. Somewhere out there, there's a job that will play to your strengths.

When we're young, most of us don't understand our strengths, and we try to bend ourselves into what we think the work environment needs. Not all strengths are right for every environment. You may possess clear artistic and creative abilities, which are valuable assets in a design firm, but of little use if you're a claims adjuster. The recruiter and hiring manager should determine this during the interview process, but they don't always get it right. Ideally, that's why you don't land every job you apply for, even if you dress right and come armed with a great resume. Here's an example of a time when it worked the way it was supposed to:

> *My daughter had just finished a degree in writing, art, and history. In college, she had part-time campus jobs in university development and fundraising. When she moved to Portland, Oregon, she couldn't immediately find any jobs that capitalized*

AVOID ROLES WHERE YOU SPEND YOUR PRECIOUS, FINITE ENERGY OVERCOMING YOUR WEAKNESSES... TO BE SUCCESSFUL AND FULFILLED AT WORK, FIND A JOB WHERE YOU HAVE A SHOT AT GREATNESS.

on her education or work experience, so she applied for a job at a retail second-hand clothing store that she frequented as a customer. To her surprise, they tested her knowledge of current fashion trends, which was almost non-existent. Her head had been full of her college work, and she hadn't thought about fashion trends during the four years she'd been in college.

She didn't get the job.

Her actual strengths weren't strengths in this particular environment. Fast forward a few years to the present day, and she's an associate editor for a magazine in the humanities. She writes content, selects articles that align with the magazine's themes, edits the magazine for publication, and leads a community storytelling fellowship. This role plays to her strengths.

Even if this is your first job and you're desperate for a paycheck, stop and ask yourself, *Does this job play to my strengths?* Or if you're well into your career and someone offers you a job at twice the salary but you know the role doesn't play to your strengths, think long and hard about how you'll spend your days and what your quality of life will be. Do you want to spend your days, your weeks, and your life with your energy zapped by daily activities where you struggle to be average?

If your job requires a significant set of strengths that you don't have, you may end up like Sisyphus, a character from Greek mythology. He was cursed to push a huge boulder to the top of the hill, only to have it roll to the bottom so that he had to push it up again, never making any progress.

STRENGTHS ARE ONLY WHAT YOU ARE GOOD AT AND WHAT YOU CARE ABOUT

I once spoke to a group of high school girls about their strengths. Which subjects did they naturally excel in—those they loved or those they didn't like?

The girls almost all responded that they were best in subjects they loved. I explained that this was important to remember. There can be inordinate pressure from parents and teachers to push you into career paths that seem safe. But you're more likely to be exceptional at those things you love. It's never worth doing something because it seems safe if you know you don't want to do that work.

Of course, no one loves every moment of the work they do, and we all will grow dozens of new skills every year. But I've worked with too many exhausted and defeated people who don't enjoy a single moment of their workday. A good rule of thumb might be 75 percent "I enjoy it" versus 25 percent "I mostly like this job, so I'll just do this because it's necessary."

THE PURSUIT OF SAFETY ISN'T ALL THAT SAFE

Remember Brian from the movie *The Breakfast Club*? He was the straight-A student who took shop class because he thought it would be easy (read "safe") because only the non-academic kids took it. He failed the class and ruined his perfect GPA and his chances for the college of his dreams because he didn't have any of the skills that made the other students good at carpentry.

Also, remember my story at the beginning of this chapter? I pursued that career mostly because it seemed safe. Lesson learned: many things that seem safe are anything but.

The safest path you can take is to follow your strengths and interests, whatever they may be, and continue to learn and grow in directions that utilize your abilities and keep you energized. STEM advocates might argue with me. Technology is the future, and they want to see more girls studying and pursuing roles in science, technology, engineering, and mathematics. They point out that girls have historically lacked exposure to math and science, and they have also been discouraged from excelling in these subjects. They rightly say we need to guide them in those directions because they are the jobs of the future.

THE SAFEST PATH YOU CAN TAKE IS TO FOLLOW YOUR STRENGTHS AND INTERESTS, WHATEVER THEY MAY BE.

Yes! By all means, let's make sure girls get that exposure, take those classes, and are encouraged to go into those fields. Let's applaud their decisions to become engineers and scientists and doctors and data analysts and software specialists—if that's what they want to do. And let's also respect the decisions of others who want to work in the humanities and arts, in the caring professions, and those who want to become makers, marketers, designers, and teachers. These days, technology has applications in every single one of these careers. And our beautiful world is crying out for dedicated, qualified people who do all these kinds of work.

So, now we have a working definition of strengths: strengths are the qualities or abilities that give you an edge over the general population and that also interest you and keep you engaged/excited.

What are yours?

YOUR UNIQUE SET OF STRENGTHS

When you want to grow in your career, it's critical to understand that you have strengths, and it's also essential to know what those strengths are. No matter who you are, you have skills that can make you stand out in a crowd. But many women have never had guidance about what their strengths might be.

One of the first steps to professional growth is to identify your strengths—those qualities that make you exceptional. (I describe exceptional as being in the top 20 percent.) Sometimes, as in the example with Carrie below, there is a startled deer-in-the-headlights response.

> *After everyone else in my workshop had shared one thing that made them exceptional, Carrie, a young woman in her early thirties, looked at me, her face blank with no hint of what she felt inside. She told the group that she'd been unable to think of any particular strengths she had. She assured us all that she was "nothing special." She said that she came to work each day and did her job as well as she could. Sure, she got solid results and positive feedback, but she was convinced that anyone could have done that.*
>
> *I sensed that Carrie needed extra encouragement to discover and embrace her strengths, so we paused at this point. I asked if she would like to set up a private call with me to explore her strengths and exceptionalness further. When we spoke a few days later, we talked about what she'd written in the Decades*

Exercise you'll see later in this chapter. After I probed a bit, this is what she told me:

Carrie had come from a poor background. She'd been the first in her family to leave her neighborhood, the first to get a college degree, and the first to hold a professional job. Over the last decade, she'd bought a house, paid it off, and was about to buy a separate rental house so she could earn passive income. She had been singled out in her current job to mentor and develop others and had won awards in the workplace for her strong customer relationships.

Carrie clearly demonstrated humility and a strong work ethic. That didn't change. These qualities were, in fact, two of her greatest strengths. But after doing this exercise, she also owned her other strengths. She knew she was personable, caring, smart, and disciplined. She persevered when others gave up. At the next workshop session, she shared those strengths with the group. And we all knew she was something special.

Why is it that so many women don't know their strengths or seem to be unable to acknowledge them? For many of us, our lives haven't guided us to be confident about our strengths. This may be because:

- Our parents, teachers, or both were quick to criticize and slow to praise, which caused us to doubt ourselves.
- We lived in a "tall poppy" culture, where we got cut down for standing tall.
- We experienced wounds from past failures that led us to believe we had no strengths.

If these resonate with you, if you've experienced one or all of them, it may be hard for you to look at your strengths head-on. However, we will explore all three of these limiting beliefs.

Withheld praise

I sat in a folding chair in the center of a circle of fifteen people who'd traveled from all over the country to attend a leadership workshop in Charlotte, North Carolina.

This was a fishbowl exercise, and it was about me. My fellow workshop participants would immediately see how I responded to something I was experiencing for the first time: feedback from people I'd worked for and with over the past few years. As Jean, the facilitator, handed pages of charts and comments to me, they were also displayed, one by one, on the screen behind me so everyone could see.

I felt calm and ready. I've always craved honest feedback, even when it's tough to hear. Yes, I felt vulnerable in front of this group, but I didn't think it would be too harsh. I could handle it.

Jean read each comment out loud, so I would hear it all and wouldn't miss a thing. As I'd guessed, there were areas I needed to work on. However, the feedback was mostly full of praise, gratitude, and care.

I was surprised and moved by what my colleagues and clients had said about me. I felt the emotion pulse up through my stomach, chest, and throat and tried not to fully take in the tributes because I was afraid I'd lose my composure in front of the group. Had I read it alone, I could have pushed past it quickly, but Jean made sure that I didn't skim over the enthusiastic comments about what made me good at my work. As I listened to her read them, tears welled up in my eyes, and my voice quivered when Jean asked me to share how it felt to hear these praises. At the end, she gently suggested that I show the results to my mother, so she would see how proud she could be of me.

And I knew that I would never do that.

While I was growing up, I don't remember my mother expressing happiness about my achievements or praise I received from others. In fact, she seemed almost worried about my good grades, awards, and positive comments. Often, she pointed out where I could have done better or worked harder. As I grew older and told her about the positive feedback I'd received, her lack of enthusiasm was obvious. I thought maybe I just needed more impressive achievements. So, I would try again. As time went on, it was unmistakable; she didn't want to hear it.

Even as an adult, I knew that if I showed the fishbowl feedback to my mother, she would nod slightly and look away, making no other comment, other than—perhaps—about how wonderful my father had been. And I'd wonder why she focused on my father, and why *I* couldn't get her affirmation or approval.

About a year before she passed away, I decided to ask my mother about this. I told her the story of the 360-feedback, Jean's suggestion that I share it with her, my decision not to, and why I decided not to. She agreed that her reaction would have been as I anticipated.

"Why is that the case?" I asked with real curiosity.

"All your life, you've wanted to be praised, and you've come back repeatedly to tell me the good things you've done. If you only knew how much I praise you to others," she said.

"But that's the thing," I said. "I don't know because you never tell me."

"You shouldn't need to hear these things," she replied. "They shouldn't need to be said. I've seen that you can be prideful, and I don't want to encourage that."

Now I had the answer to something that had confused me for my whole life. As she withheld praise, I tried harder to earn it and, more importantly, to hear it from her. The more I tried to earn her approval, the more she dug in and refused to give praise. It was a game we had played for a lifetime. Have you, too, played this game with one or more of your parents?

After years of her withholding praise, I finally understood her reasons. Those reasons had to do with her beliefs and values. She didn't think I should need validation. On some level, she thought that offering approval would inflame a character flaw she saw in me.

However, this lifelong dance had the opposite effect on me. I'm embarrassed to say this, but I became an unabashed approval-seeker. Too often, my efforts were about hearing approval from others that I never got at home. At the same time, I had an ever-present sense of shame when I shared my accomplishments with others. Yes, I could see there were good things I'd done, but I knew it was wrong to talk about them.

Culture of cut-downs

You might come from a culture in which tall poppies get cut down, and it could come from your family or your community. This enforced humility is common in Australia, where I spent thirty years. Janice (below) learned it, as well, when she moved to the UK. This can confuse an outsider who may not realize that the person who picks on you may also want to be your friend.

> *Janice, an international banking consultant, had an adjustment to make when she moved from Chicago to London. At her new workplace, even among professionals, it was common to put a new colleague through a unique form of hazing that consisted of teasing and small put-downs. In her case, they teased her for her accent and occasional mispronunciations, created the nickname "Genial Janice" because she was always trying to be pleasant, and ribbed her about "typical American" ideas she introduced in meetings.*
>
> *She shared concerns about this with her British husband, who said with affection, "Don't you understand? That means they like you. What you want to worry about is if they* don't *tease you; then they're probably talking about you behind your back."*

Janice gradually came to recognize this as part of the British sense of humor and culture in her workplace, and she learned to accept it, even if she never quite understood it.

There are more serious cut-down cultures. In certain communities, people often harbor a genuine antagonism toward success, especially when the person is also affluent. Your working-class family may resent you for pursuing a college education or for leaving your hometown. Gangs sometimes target those who leave their ranks to find a better life. It

YOU'VE HEARD THAT FAILURE IS A NECESSARY PART OF SUCCESS. BUT THAT DOESN'T MAKE IT EASIER WHEN YOU EXPERIENCE IT, ESPECIALLY WHEN THE FAILURE IS VERY PERSONAL.

can even happen with people you don't know, like trolls on the internet who are determined to bring down a successful person or business for the smallest reason. It takes a lot of determination to continue when others want to take you down a notch.

Failures we can't forget

Finally, we might find it hard to acknowledge our strengths because we've experienced failures that left us raw and wounded. Almost everyone can remember at least one failure that really knocked their confidence.

You've heard that failure is a necessary part of success. But that doesn't make it easier when you experience it, especially when the failure is very personal.

Nour had qualified to be a physician in Lebanon, but she couldn't practice in the US because of the multitude of requirements to secure a residency slot. Her husband had a job in the US, but the family needed some extra money to live comfortably, so Nour accepted a job managing medical records. The software was new to her, and with only basic English skills, she struggled to learn it. She made several mistakes in the first few months and lost her job. She felt a burning sense of shame that she'd failed. Even though she'd always loved medicine, she decided to stay home to look after her children and consider a job later. It took her four years to work up the courage to apply for another job.

Four years. The sooner we can reframe failure, the better. But how do we do that?

FIND THE COURAGE TO EMBRACE FAILURE

When people take the Values in Action (VIA) Character Strengths Survey (you'll hear more about this in a bit), one strength that comes up on occasion is bravery. When that happens, I smile and say, "After years of this work, I know that bravery always has a story behind it. Something happened in your life that required you to be brave, and you stepped up to it."

We aren't born brave; you'll know that if you've ever seen a new baby. We are made brave by the situations life throws at us and our decision to face them.

Bravery is often related to experiences we normally associate with failure and the work it takes to move past that failure. A few examples could be:

- You were fired from a much-needed job but found another, better job.
- You made a poor investment decision that resulted in the loss of financial security, but you managed to rebuild your net worth.
- A spouse passed away without providing for you, and you had to scramble to make a living and support the family.

Maya was one of the youngest team leaders in the tech division of her company. When she looked at her key performance indicators (KPIs), she thought she was doing a great job, driving solid results in her area. When the organization ran a company-wide engagement survey, however, she had some of the lowest engagement scores across the board. Unfortunately for Maya, team engagement was a KPI she'd discounted. She thought the other results were more important. Her bonus was reduced, and she received counseling from her manager to fix this.

Angry at the unfair system, she initially blamed the low scores on her predecessor, but as she read the results more closely, she could see they pointed directly at her. It was clear that she didn't listen to her team, didn't empower them, and didn't appreciate them. Always an achiever, Maya took this revelation as a challenge, found a coach, and worked hard to become a better leader. Her team engagement immediately improved. Within two years, her scores were some of the highest in the company. She was proud of the change, and leading people became the most important and satisfying part of her job.

What makes stories of overcoming failure most impactful is not that these bad things happened, but that these women moved past them and got to the other side—a process that can often be slow, messy, and painful. But these overcomers didn't curl up to protect their soft underbellies. A woman committed to growth allows failure to teach her what she needs to learn so she can become the leader she wants to be.

Failure, if we learn from it, can liberate us to live without constant feelings of anxiety and fear. Whatever we're afraid of can be best overcome by facing it.

WAYS TO EXPLORE YOUR STRENGTHS

You'll deal better with everything if you're clear about your strengths. I've seen countless women sit up straighter, and I've seen their eyes shine with confidence when they allow themselves to clarify and focus on their strengths. Let's work on a few different ways to discover your strengths.

1. List your life's achievements

I used to ask my clients to consider their life achievements. They often drew a complete blank, or I got vague and generic responses that ignored whole swaths of their lives. So, I came up with this approach, the Decades Exercise, to help them remember achievements they might have forgotten.

The Decades Exercise

To do this, you'll need to look at your life in a way you may not have considered before. If you're reading this book, you're probably at least in your twenties. That means you're into your third decade. Other readers will be further along than that.

Life achievements come gradually, and it's easy to suffer from what is called the "recency effect." That's when you only recall achievements from your recent past.

In contrast, this exercise asks you to remember the good things you did as a child, as a young adult, and in the following decades. It will help you dig for gold in your personal history.

1. Settle in and give yourself thirty minutes or so of reflection time. Think of times that you've had success in your life, either individually or as part of a team, for each decade of your life. The successes can be professional or personal.
2. Start with your school days, considering sports achievements, friendships forged, honors conferred, speeches presented—you get the idea.
3. Then, keep going, decade-by-decade, so you don't miss significant events you've forgotten about.

If you do this work honestly and remember your whole life, you'll probably come up with dozens of achievements.

A couple of things to note as you walk down memory lane:

- An achievement that was a big deal when you were ten years old—an award at school, a part in a play, a home run when it was needed, or a perfect clarinet solo at a concert—might not seem worthy of mention, but these are the events that built your confidence, talents, and recognition, and they set a direction for future pursuits.

- There may be some periods you want to avoid remembering. But when you refuse to look back, you can miss the richness of your growth. You may have had dark times, and it can feel painful to revisit those times—perhaps a marriage ended in misery, you had addiction problems, or you lost someone close. If you look squarely at these trials, you may find that those painful experiences were the crucibles that shaped your character and strength.

Charlotte was a well-educated, warm, and confident director of an international nonprofit that provided aid to women and families. She told me about a long period in her thirties when she'd stayed in a marriage with a deeply depressed alcoholic and gambling addict. She hid it from most people, but she found she needed to work in small, manageable roles while she tried to help her husband, provide for her family, and protect her young children and herself.

After a while, Charlotte realized that her husband wasn't getting better. If she and her children were to have a future, she needed to leave and separate emotionally and financially from him. Once she did that, she was able to blossom at work and quickly grow professionally.

"Being in that relationship—and leaving—was harder than anything my work could have thrown at me!" she said. But it made her resilient and resourceful because she had to lean on herself. And she went from strength to strength at work, rising steadily to the top.

Even recent achievements can be hard to take credit for if you don't take a breath and look at your life. Maybe last year, you initiated a major change at work that was a big success or started a regular gym workout or were accepted to graduate school.

When you see how far you've come during your entire life, you can gain confidence to continue your achievements in the future and move toward new accomplishments.

Here's a sample list from a forty-five-year-old:

Early and teen years

- Won an award for my math skills
- Got a lead role in the school play
- Was accepted as an exchange student and lived overseas for three months
- Was selected to be in an award-winning marching band
- Was accepted to my first-choice college

Twenties

- Finished my degree while working part-time
- Was elected as an officer in my college/university club

- Worked as a camp counselor during the summers
- Landed my first professional role and got promoted
- Started graduate school
- Got married and planned the wedding so it was exactly what I wanted

Thirties

- Left a safe job to do work I cared about
- Had children and managed the challenges of juggling work and family
- Joined a gym and got an award for most improved
- Successfully ran my first big project and led a team
- Bought a home and made it beautiful
- Learned to garden
- Completed graduate school

Forties

- Bounced back after being laid off in a restructure
- Moved to another city for a great new job
- Introduced and ran a major business change at my new company
- Joined Toastmasters and became a strong public speaker
- Took up painting as a serious hobby

Now, make your list. Obviously, if you're younger, you'll have fewer decades to work with, but you may be surprised at how many peak achievements you can find.

Find your strengths from your peak performances

In the example list above, what strengths did you glean? Did you see willingness to change, collaboration, determination, hard work, leadership, organization, creativity, resilience, managing multiple roles, influence, and courage?

Now, notice what you've learned from your painful times and their recovery periods. Embrace that growth. Reframe those stories to see the muscle you've developed. Instead of viewing them as dark moments of your past, let them become part of your journey. Your life is a work of art. You've crafted it with each step—and misstep—at a time.

When you've completed this exercise, you may choose to validate it with someone else who knows you well. They can probably see strengths that you haven't thought of or have taken for granted. Or have them do the exercise for themselves, too, and share your results with each other.

A note about trauma: if you have trauma in your past that could come back to haunt you during this exercise, you may want to focus only on the positive aspects of your achievements. Or, if you are working with a professional, you could ask to do the exercise with your therapist, so you will be in a safe space. If you're not working with a professional, you might consider starting. There are so many therapeutic modes that deal with trauma. It could be a good time to get the help you need, so you can move with confidence into your future.

2. Strengths instruments

After you've played the archaeologist of your past, there's another way to further investigate your strengths—through an online strengths-finding test. Some surveys have a basic free version that can take anywhere from ten to forty minutes to complete. Almost all offer a paid version that you can use to deepen your awareness of yourself.

Strengths instruments help you see good things about yourself that you might completely overlook. Because they're based on research, they can help you view your positive qualities more objectively. The one I frequently use with clients was developed by Martin Seligman—who's been called the father of positive psychology—and others at the VIA (Values in Action) Institute.

The VIA Character Strengths Survey is both simple and intuitive, yet it also draws from a strong research base. It's a free instrument that takes ten to twenty minutes to complete and provides rich results. If you'd like, you can also purchase the paid version, which offers ideas on how to utilize your strengths most effectively.

What I love about this instrument is its emphasis on character. Character is incredibly important in leadership, and I appreciate the way it shows how each of us has a completely different bundle of top character strengths.

In their book *The Extraordinary Leader*, John Zenger and Joseph Folkman likened character strengths to the center pole of an old-style circus tent. The other poles that make up the tent can represent your other strengths—maybe your ability to speak or write well, your numerical or analytical skills, your ability to organize or problem-solve—and they all give the tent its unique shape. However, without the center pole to support them, they'll collapse in on themselves and eventually fall to the ground. You want to take time to develop other strengths that are valuable in your workplace. Too often, most leaders don't spend much time or thought on their character.

Your character is central to how you lead yourself and how you lead others. Every great leader you know, have read about, or heard of has brought their essential character to their role. Everyone has a slightly different way of showing their character. Think of the difference between Winston Churchill and Mother Theresa. Both were great leaders in vastly different ways.

You also have your way, and taking a character-strengths survey can help you explore more about yourself. There isn't one right or wrong way to demonstrate character, but there's a way that is meaningful for you.

THE ELEPHANT IN THE ROOM QUESTION

We've been considering the importance of your strengths. But what about your weaknesses? For many, it may not feel right or healthy or humble to focus on your strengths. If that's true for you, you may try to wriggle out of the strengths exercises I've suggested by saying that you've learned much more from your weaknesses. I get it; I felt the same way.

I'd been a coach for about five years when I first heard the phrase "strengths-based coaching," a concept from the positive psychology movement that quickly took root in the professional development community. I was not a fan and, therefore, was not an early adopter.

At that time, my approach to coaching had been to focus on what my clients needed to change, and then to help them change it. This meant that they got quite a lot of not-so-positive feedback. In a way, I'm surprised they put up with it. But my clients were generally very senior in their organizations, with strong track records of success, and were more confident than a junior person in corporate life. They'd received plenty of feedback in the past about their weaknesses and usually weren't afraid to hear about them from me. I even (and I cringe a little when I say this) used to tell prospective clients that I was good at "hitting someone over the head with a two-by-four." (This was a metaphor, in case you're wondering). And so, we worked together to find and fix their weaknesses, and we got pretty good results.

However, as I read and learned and listened, I began to believe that strengths-based coaching works better. Why? Great leaders are never perfect—no exceptions—nor are they expected to be. They are expected to be effective. They are expected to get results and to lead people well, so they can also get results.

Somewhere along the way, some people—particularly women—get it in their heads that they need to be perfect. They try to keep their inboxes to zero, write email masterpieces, never stumble while presenting, or some other nice-to-have quality that doesn't make much of a difference. In their book *How Women Rise,* Sally Helgesen and Marshall Goldsmith identify twelve habits that hold women back at work. Habit seven is called "The Perfection Trap." The authors identify reasons why women need to stop themselves from falling into this trap. They say that perfectionism:

- Creates stress, both for you and the people who work with you because perfectionism is not sustainable.
- Keeps you focused on details when you need to pay attention to strategic and big-picture issues.
- Can cause you to be annoyed or bothered by all the things that go wrong—and things will always go wrong, at least some of the time.
- Creates disappointment and a negative mindset.

We don't have to be perfect, and it's not even possible. The strengths-based approach promoted by Zenger and Folkman tells us that we only need to stand out in three to five areas to be perceived as exceptional leaders. Those could include (for example) problem-solving, initiative, relationship-building, persistence, and integrity. For the rest, we can settle for proficiency.

Of course, you don't want to be terrible at anything you do. That's a recipe for disaster. Sometimes, you may need to move from weak to proficient in areas that are critical for your job. That's important, but remember that it won't get you to greatness. For excellence to emerge, you need to become even better than you already are. You need to go from good to great.

So, the answer is that you don't want to ignore

THE STRENGTHS-BASED APPROACH TELLS US THAT WE ONLY NEED TO STAND OUT IN THREE TO FIVE AREAS TO BE PERCEIVED AS EXCEPTIONAL LEADERS... FOR THE REST, WE CAN SETTLE FOR PROFICIENCY.

your weaknesses. But sometimes good enough is good enough. Your strengths are the path to extraordinary performance.

BRINGING IT ALL TOGETHER

You've now explored your strengths, perhaps in ways you've never considered before.

First: You looked at your peak achievements through the different stages of your life, from a trembling but talented schoolgirl's first role in a play to making the track team that went to State, right up to nailing the project that received management accolades last month.

Chances are, you noticed some trends when you looked at your strengths over time. You saw how you overcame adversity, learned, grew, and got better as your experience expanded. Those trends are perfect strengths cues; pay attention to them.

Second: You've taken advantage of an online strengths instrument (such as the VIA Character Strengths Survey or another strengths survey) to give you a more objective view of your actual strengths. A list of instruments and how to find them is shown in Appendix 1.

Towering strengths

You now have ample material to pull together a list of your top five strengths. You can call these your "towering strengths," a term borrowed from the Center for Creative Leadership. These are five areas in which you are exceptional, better than most other people. These five strengths give you your professional and personal edge.

After you've done the work, you may find it challenging to limit your strengths to five. The reality is that you may have many more, so why narrow your list to five? Because it's important to effortlessly remember these, and most of us can't readily remember more than five things at a time. You'll want to:

- Remember your strengths for yourself so you can think about how to use them on a current project or your team's upcoming strategy session.

- Remember your strengths so you can put your hand up to contribute in a unique way to your work and life. Find ways to use your strengths in all you do, whether organizing an event, speaking up with courage, or leading better outcomes on your team.

- Remember your strengths so you can share them with your manager at your next performance review with examples of what you've done and what you'd like to do more of in the future.

- Remember your strengths so you can respond with confidence at your next job interview (and back them up with some good examples). One of the most common interview questions is, "What strengths will you bring to this role?" If you know this answer in advance, you'll avoid that awkward silence. You won't freeze up. You'll speak with the confidence that comes from knowing yourself.

- List your five towering strengths on paper. Put these somewhere you can see them. I suggest that you write them on the inside back page of whatever notebook you use regularly. If you work from home, put them up where you can see them from your desk and validate them daily.

Now that you've answered the question, "What are my strengths?" we'll look at a new question: "What do I want to stand for?"

RISE BECAUSE YOU STAND FOR SOMETHING

If you don't stand for something, you will fall for anything.

—Peter Marshall,
Chaplain to the US Senate (1947)

'VE WORKED WITH many leaders and had the opportunity to observe some extraordinary careers. Looking back, there was one slightly obscure quality that seemed to help these women and men move up through the ranks more quickly and successfully than their colleagues. That quality was what they stood for at work. The most successful leaders stood for something they believed was truly important.

You know what surprised me? It didn't really matter what they stood for, but the fact that they stood for *something* was important. It was very different for different leaders. Some examples were:

- A higher purpose for the business—healing people, fixing a societal problem, creating financial safety
- New, innovative ideas that hadn't been tried before
- Personal/professional growth for the people who work for them
- Community contribution—ensuring the business was connected locally
- Integrity of business processes, like solid and ethical supply chains
- Customer-centered product design
- A great customer experience
- Sustainable business practices
- Great teams that were productive, happy, and collaborative

What they stood for usually aligned with the functional area where that leader worked, but that wasn't always the case. They cared about all issues in the business, including bottom-line results, but there was often one issue or one platform they chose to stand for. And they stood for it publicly. Whenever that topic came up, that leader was the person others thought of.

Contrast that to those who bend and change with whatever is on-trend in their business. They think they're there to stand for business success or even business growth, but those ideas are vague and amorphous.

Whatever you stand for needs to be specific and proactive. And it needs to be something that lights you up.

WHAT DO YOU STAND FOR AT WORK?

This topic hasn't made its way into business research or writing. But if you listen to interviews with highly successful businesspeople, you'll realize there's always something that underpins the story of their success. There are no classes in "what I want to stand for" in traditional educational environments. For some people, what they stand for comes almost by accident. Take Neil's story, below.

WHATEVER YOU STAND FOR NEEDS TO BE SPECIFIC AND PROACTIVE. AND IT NEEDS TO BE SOMETHING THAT LIGHTS YOU UP.

Neil, a new client, had a warm smile and an accent that placed his origins from northern England. Humble, soft-spoken, and kind, he worked as head of risk in an institutional bank where aggression and hyper-ambition were the norm. Before meeting Neil, I imagined that the top risk person would be highly analytical and would need to be super-tough to face the fiercely driven dealmakers I'd come across at the bank.

However, Neil didn't fit my expectations. He was genuinely more focused on people than on numbers. He cared about the team he led. When he dealt with his ambitious colleagues, he was always respectful. Neil came across a bit like Columbo from the detective series. Maybe he was the smartest guy in the room, but he would never let anyone know it. He guided outcomes with quiet, intelligent questions and logic, with strong values beneath all that he did and said.

When I asked Neil how he decided to become a risk manager in such a competitive environment, he smiled and told me this story:

"When I was a teenager, I had a friend who lived with his grandparents near my family. Out of nowhere (it seemed to me), they had to sell their house and move out of our nice village to a small home in an area where no one would choose to live. Everyone expressed sadness about what had happened to them. I asked my parents what that was.

"It turned out they'd been victims of a fraud that had affected thirty-two thousand people in the UK. Robert Maxwell, the head of a publishing empire, had 'borrowed' the pension funds of his employees to cover his personal debts. By the time it was discovered, the money was gone, and the pensions couldn't be recovered. Robert Maxwell committed suicide, but a lot of other people were implicated in the fraud. In the end, not a single person went to jail.

"I couldn't believe this was possible in England. I wanted to do something about it, so I pursued a career in financial surveillance, then transitioned into compliance and risk management. I never forgot what I was there to do. I wanted to make sure that what had happened to those thirty-two thousand people would never happen to anyone again."

And that is what Neil stood for.

Not everyone has epiphanies like this during their teenage years. At best, during our teens and twenties, most of us don't figure out what we want to do but what we don't want to do. We're not quite ready to stand for anything other than a paycheck—and the bigger the better.

However, whether you're twenty-five or sixty-five, if you have a job, there's an opportunity to stop and think about what you want to stand for. It'll help you find or create work that matters, and you'll be happier and more successful because of it.

How to answer the question for yourself

Let me show you a step-by-step approach that will help you uncover what you want to stand for at work. Ultimately, you'll be able to develop a short, clear statement with the help of the formula below:

Strengths x Values x Passions = What I stand for at work

In Strategy 1, you identified your strengths. Now, you will clarify your values, identify your passions, and craft a statement of what you stand for.

Clarifying your values can change your career

During one of our online group sessions, Bronte, a young woman in her early thirties, looked at the rest of the group with shining eyes. Although none of us had met in person, we could feel her excitement across the screen as she explained what had happened since our last session.

Bronte had worked in change management at a national supermarket chain during her twelve-year career. Change management in any business is crucial work, and Bronte excelled at it. But she was somewhat frustrated that others had already decided what the business change should be, and she didn't always get to work on projects that aligned with her values. Bronte yearned for that alignment, and she'd worked hard to identify her strengths, values, and passions at work.

What she constructed as her personal statement was simple and true: "I am passionate about making business changes that improve the customer and employee experience."

A month later, Bronte heard a presentation by Liam, an executive she'd never met. He spoke about a new business unit he was building from the ground up. It was a unit designed to improve both customer and employee experiences. He said his vision for the team was to be a village—a community where every member shared a common intention to make internal processes smoother and service better for both customers and employees. Bronte had goose bumps: these were the exact changes she wanted to create and build, and she made up her mind to be part of that village.

She canvassed her contacts to find someone who would recommend her to Liam and found two colleagues who knew him. Because of their experience with Bronte, they suggested that he consider her for his team. He agreed to interview her, and at the interview, he asked why she wanted to be part of this effort. She was ready for that question and told him how she'd dug deep to think about the kind of work she wanted to do and the kind of impact she wanted to have. She even pulled out her personal statement and read it to him.

Bronte was appointed to be one of the heads of the new business unit. This was a promotion for her, and she could do work she deeply cared about.

Why values are so important

Many people—perhaps most—have never taken the time to clarify their values. Why would they need to? The company they work for has already done it, and all they need to do is fall into line with what has already been stated.

Organizations of all shapes and sizes recognize the importance of having clear, publicly stated values. True, there are some companies in which value statements are empty words, but others take their values very seriously, and for good reasons.

- **Values bring people together.** They give people a common language, a shared moral compass, and a sense of purpose. Robert Cialdini, in his book *Influence*, says that unity is one of the most powerful ways to influence groups. Values create a sense of unity.

- **Values guide individual behavior within the organization.** When values are clearly stated and accepted by all, people can check their behavior through the lens of their organization's values. And they can call out the behavior of others if they see a lack of alignment.
- **Values guide leadership decisions.** Together with strategy, values can be a touchstone for every decision. Does this decision support our values? If there's a conflict, it needs to be reexamined and rethought.

However, your company's values, as good as they may be, might be different from your values. One obvious example relates to your personal and family relationships. Many people identify "family focus" (or similar phrases) as their top value. However, family focus is rarely a core organizational value. Organizations tend to focus on words like teamwork, achievement, innovation, and collaboration—values that support the organization's productivity, harmonious relationships, and competitive edge.

Does this mean that you should let go of your value of family focus while you are at work? Not at all. You aren't owned by the company you work for, which is why the term "human capital" is objectionable, but that's a separate rant. As an individual, you need to own your life; therefore, you need to be guided by your most important needs and beliefs. And it's important to take the time and energy to get clear about what they are. Why?

- **Values bring *you* together.** They bring you into alignment with yourself. Too often, the demands of your work and personal life may be in competition. This could cause the lines to blur about what's important. Clearly stating your values provides a moral compass and a sense of purpose. You'll be more likely to speak up when you see something going wrong. You'll be better equipped to advocate for what is right.

- **Values guide *your* behavior.** With a clearly stated set of values, you can see what the next step should be. For example, if your personal values include health or well-being, that value can guide you in a very tangible way. It can help you make a choice to stop where you are and go for that lunchtime walk instead of grabbing a candy bar so you can get a sugar boost to keep going.

- **Values guide *your* leadership decisions.** As a leader at work, your values might provide you with a way to check your interactions and decisions with your team, your peers, and your manager. At home, they can help guide your co-leadership as you make decisions with your partner and with your family.

> AS AN INDIVIDUAL, YOU NEED TO OWN YOUR LIFE; THEREFORE, IT'S ESSENTIAL FOR YOU TO BE GUIDED BY YOUR MOST IMPORTANT NEEDS AND BELIEFS.

How to identify your values

So, how can you determine your values? It might be helpful to have a values list to work from. Try an online search, and you'll see that others have done some of the hard work for you.

You can also use an inexpensive values instrument, such as the Personal Values Assessment from the Barrett Values Centre (link in Appendix 1); this is a very quick way to identify your top ten values. They also provide a mini-course that can help you explore the deeper meaning of your values and consider how to rely on them.

Here's an easy, free way: Brené Brown has some of the most-watched TED talks of all time, a popular podcast, and she's the author of several New York Times bestsellers, which include *Dare to Lead*.

As part of a free online program, she and her team have compiled more than one hundred values that you can access, use, and add to. You can find a link in Appendix 2.

Ken Blanchard, the bestselling author of *The One-Minute Manager*, speaks about the importance of values in his blog, *How We Lead*. He suggests that you list all the most important values you can think of (you could use Brené Brown's list to help you get started), and then gradually hone them down. When you compare one against the others, is it more or less important? You continue to trim the list until you get to three to five values. When you get there, these are your core values. They may evolve over time, but if you've put in the effort and searched within yourself, you'll find they won't change dramatically.

Below are my core values, which I generated using Ken Blanchard's approach approximately twenty-five years ago after hearing him speak at a conference. My top five were:

- Integrity
- Love
- Health
- Achievement
- Fun

Blanchard also suggests that you create your definition for each value by filling in the blank on this statement:

I know I'm acting in alignment with this value when (fill in the blank).

For example, *I know I'm acting with integrity when I can say with confidence that I'm doing the right thing for the right reason.*

These five values worked beautifully for me for many years. I used them to guide me through the small and big decisions in my life. They helped me through some difficult times—divorce, parental challenges, financial decisions, and negotiations with clients. They guided me in my personal life and my work by asking questions like these:

- Am I "in integrity" with this action or decision?
- Does it come from a place of love (for myself, family, friends, community, environment)?
- Does it show care for my health and the health of those I love? (Note: health is a value that enables everything else. Without health, so many wonderful things aren't possible.)

- Is this action on the path to the achievement I've committed to?
- Finally, does this action have a sense of fun to it?

This last value has brought a lightness and brightness to my life that has made it richer and more enjoyable. Sure, not every moment can be fun, but if life isn't fun for a long time, pay attention. Something may not be right.

After a while, I noticed that my values had subtly changed. The first two, integrity and love, hadn't changed, but the last three had evolved into new versions of themselves.

- **Health evolved into wellbeing**. Beyond physical health, this value expanded to physical, mental, emotional, and spiritual dimensions.
- **Achievement evolved into making a difference**. I realized that success isn't about achievement for its own sake. I now wanted to focus on doing work that would make others' lives better.
- **Fun evolved into joy**. Fun was very important to my younger self, but as I grew older, I realized that joy had a more peaceful, centered aspect to it. But I still love to laugh until my sides hurt!

You may find that there's considerable overlap between your strengths and your values. That's not a coincidence. When you focus, over time, on living in alignment with a particular value, it is likely to become a strength.

Access your passion

Now, let's look at passion. There have been considerable arguments about whether people should pursue their passions. Many are skeptical about whether it's possible or useful, and they see passion pursuit as a path to disappointment. I'm using the word "passion" to mean anything that excites or interests you. It doesn't have to mean finding a career in surfing or mountain climbing, although it may, as many REI employees can attest.

Yvonne Chouinard also managed to access his passion for the outdoors when he founded Patagonia in 1973. He started the company because of his personal love for rock climbing and his desire to prove that business could be ethical *and* successful. Patagonia has pioneered the use of sustainable materials, fair labor practices, and corporate environmental activism. There is little doubt that it has been successful, with three thousand employees in 2024 and revenues that exceeded $1 billion.

Most of us opt for a different path, spending our days at work and pursuing passions in our spare time. Is this enough? We still need to consider our interests. Who doesn't want to be able to do work that excites and interests them?

Here's how Andrea brought her career to life by asking important passion questions.

> *Andrea, in her early forties, was funny and personable, and she described herself as a great team player and collaborator. As a marketing manager at a major pharmaceutical company, she had a long list of achievements and a happy team.*

But something didn't feel quite right. She hadn't been promoted in a while. Her career had stalled for no apparent reason, and she felt pigeonholed. She said, "I see people being promoted to roles I know I could do just as well—probably better, if I'm honest with myself." Andrea felt that she was in a holding pattern, and she thought her only choice was to leave her company to find a new job.

When I interviewed more senior managers about Andrea, one manager said, "I see her as a safe pair of hands. Give her something to do, and she'll do it well. Her people are happy. To me, it seems like she's in exactly the right role."

As Andrea's coach, I gently pointed out what a backhanded compliment this was. To be called a "safe pair of hands" is the work equivalent of being called a "nice person." It's good to be nice, but it's not very exciting. It's good to be a safe pair of hands, but it doesn't exactly make you sound like a dynamic, proactive leader. If Andrea wanted to be seen differently—to be seen as a force in the business—she needed to demonstrate what she stood for.

We worked on her values and strengths. But when I asked her about what she felt passionate about in her work, she drew a blank. It wasn't about great marketing strategies and product launches. She'd managed those for years.

I asked her to list fifty things she'd like to be, do, or try as part of the rest of her career. Her eyes widened at the number. "Fifty?" she asked. I pointed out that over the next ten years, she'd be asked by her employer to do things differently, again and again. There was little doubt that she would be, do, or try fifty new approaches, actions, or projects in that period. This was her chance to imagine what she'd *like those new things to be.*

She brought her list to the next session with obvious excitement. What she'd seen from her list was that she cared deeply about the company's end users—the patients and their families—even though she had little direct contact with them in her current role. She wanted to understand them and influence the

*way her company thought about them. She wanted to make cus-
tomers' lives better through the products they introduced to the
market.*

*As a marketing manager, she knew how to make products
more attractive to customers, but she'd never actually thought
about how to be an advocate for customers. This was a leap she
was excited to make.*

*This was Andrea's passion, which had been lying dormant
beneath her day-to-day competence. She had what she needed
to create her personal statement: "To be the voice of the customer as we market our products."*

*She got permission for her team to identify and work
directly with some end users of the products, thus creating a
marketing program around close, continuous personal contact. Marketing became an expression of what the team learned
there, and they were able to adapt their approaches.*

Asking Passion Questions

At this point, you know your strengths, and you've clarified
your values. Now, let's supercharge them with your passion.

In this section, you'll answer a few questions that will help
you access your positive emotions and energy:

Question 1: What challenge makes you feel excited?

Someone asks you to do something, fix something, or lead
something. And when they do, it makes your blood pump (in
a good way). Are you a problem solver? Do you love to create
powerful events? Do you thrive when you're leading people?

Question 2: Over the years, what has made you happiest at work?

What work have you done in the past that's brought you joy or pleasure? I often ask clients to think of a job (not their current role) that brought them joy or pleasure. These can be wonderful passion clues—the chance to work on a team that delivered great results, the satisfaction of teaching something you know, the pure pleasure of serving customers. Take note of these.

I once worked with a group of mid-level attorneys in a prestigious law firm, and as an icebreaker, I asked each participant to share what previous job they'd most enjoyed. The responses were rich with clues about what brought them meaning at work.

Anna had enjoyed her college job as a nursing home aide. She loved to listen to the elderly residents' stories and to find ways to make them feel comfortable and content. Anna could have decided to work in estate law, where she would work with older people to help them ensure their end-of-life wishes were honored.

Erica had grown up in a musical family and had been in a band. She loved the stimulation of being around performers and other creative people. Erica could have worked in entertainment law.

Steve had worked on a political campaign throughout his college years. He had loved the opportunity to listen to people's views and persuade them to consider his candidate. Steve could have worked in politics, but his love for persuasion could mean that he would enjoy many types of legal practice.

What clues can you find in roles you've most enjoyed in your past?

Question 3. *What really lights your fire?*

What would you love to achieve through your work? What are fifty things you'd like to be, do, or try at work over the next ten years?

If there were no barriers, would you want to:

- Help other women be successful?
- Make a positive impact on the environment?
- Solve knotty business problems?
- Lead a project that's a game-changer for your business?
- Attract a more diverse workforce?
- Work on an acquisition for your company?
- Start up a new "greenfields" project?
- Work overseas with your company?

What else?

Don't worry if you're not yet engaged in the work you'd love to do. Most large businesses will have opportunities for you to dip your toe in the water, either through projects or committees.

If you don't see an opportunity in your business, ask around. You could also get training, take a class, do volunteer work, or join an association. As you take those actions, you can put them on your resume and your work profile, becoming better positioned to do what you love.

This takes time, yes, but you can often include these as part of your day job. What's the upside? Let's go back to Andrea. She did some research about how to engage customers and took classes to learn a methodology she thought would work for the company. She continuously advocated for customers in her approach to marketing. Ultimately, the company recognized the value of this approach, and Andrea was appointed as the chief marketing officer, where she was able to create change across every division.

Your personal statement

Now you have the input to write your personal statement that will codify what you want to stand for at work. Here are a few tips:

- Keep it simple, so it's memorable, and you can commit it to your memory—and your heart.
- Check to see if it makes you feel something. Is it meaningful to you? When you read it, do you feel authenticity and emotion?
- You need to be able to apply it. Have you had to make a difficult work/life decision in the past six months? How might your personal statement have guided you to make that decision? How could your statement help you with the decisions that are ahead of you?

Here are some examples from my past clients.

- *I bring people together to accomplish (x) and have fun while they do it.*
- *I find the stories that are hidden in the data.*
- *I keep customers front and center in everything my team does.*
- *I create practical innovations that help employees do their jobs.*
- *I eliminate bureaucracy and make work simple.*

- *I bring new perspectives and solve problems others believe can't be solved.*
- *I find ways AI can make things easier for our customers.*
- *I en + courage: I want to help others have courage in themselves.*

How to use it

Your personal statement can serve as a true north in your work life. You don't have to share it with anyone to let it guide you, but there can be benefits in communicating it to others.

Once you know what you want to stand for at work, you can use the statement in many ways, such as:

- Share it in job interviews.
- Use it as part of an introduction to your team, either as a member or a leader.
- Share it with your manager in a performance review.
- Use it as a check-in when you're uncomfortable. (Is it possible you've been pulled off your path?)
- Identify like-minded people—people who are in alignment with your personal statement—to work with and projects you'd like to work on.
- Align your actions with your statement every day, so you can do more of what's important to you and less of what is not.

You'll find many opportunities to use your statement as we go through this book. It's the foundation of a thriving career.

RISE AND BE SEEN

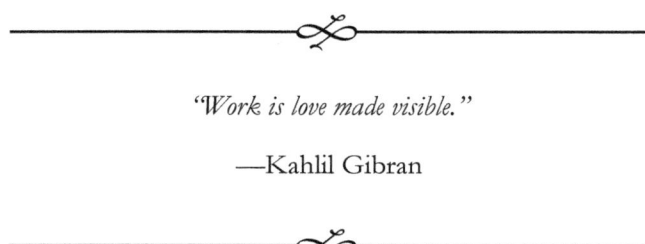

"Work is love made visible."

—Kahlil Gibran

MANY OF US cling to the idea that hard work alone should be enough to help us get ahead. But that's not the way the working world operates. Most organizations strive to maintain a level playing field. But keeping our heads down and plugging away in a dark corner is never enough, and it never has been. That's true whether you're male or female.

David was a mid-level manager in his late thirties, working for one of Australia's largest banks. He came to his first coaching session with his finger ready to push the exit button. He'd already spoken to HR and let them know about his plan to leave, and they'd asked him to meet with me for a few coaching sessions before he took action. He agreed but didn't hold out much hope.

Here's the story he told me:

David had worked for the bank for seven years. They'd moved him to a role in their global headquarters, and he'd steadily moved up. He was seen as a strong performer and an exceptional people leader.

He applied for a job that had been advertised internally at the bank as a senior role in a division located in his home state. It would be a promotion and a natural progression for him. He easily met the job criteria and was highly qualified in every way. Someone even joked that the post looked like it had been secretly written for him. The interview went well, and he felt confident that he was on his way.

But he didn't get the job. And he found out in the worst possible way. The person who got the job mentioned it to him in passing. No one had told David that he hadn't been successful. To make matters worse, the colleague who'd gotten the role was far less qualified than David was. When David asked for feedback about why he didn't get the role, it didn't make sense to him, not even close.

In our session, he spread out his performance reviews (all top-notch) across the table and showed me his 360-degree feedback from colleagues, which was also positive.

"What do you see here?" he asked me. "Do you see any reason I missed out on this job?"

I had to admit that I didn't. David was gutted, humiliated, hurt, and ready to walk out. However, he agreed to meet again the following week, so I could gather more information and we could explore it further.

I read through his performance reviews and spoke to the head of talent, but she couldn't shed light on this decision. Still, something in this situation niggled at me, although I couldn't figure out what it was.

Before our next session, I woke up in the middle of the night, and out of nowhere, I knew what had happened. And when we met again, I broke the coach's code: rather than asking questions, I blurted out my insight. I said, "I think I know why the other guy got the job. I've worked with leaders in this company for a long time, and I've heard of him a lot. He speaks in front of groups, and people have mentioned him to me. Everybody knows who he is. But until I met you, I'd never heard of you."

I took a deep breath and said, "I think you might be invisible."

VISIBILITY IS ONE OF THE REASONS PEOPLE ARE PROMOTED AND GIVEN CAREER-BUILDING ROLES.

If your career isn't moving as fast as you'd like, you may—like David—be invisible in your organization. You do a good job and wait to be acknowledged with a raise and a promotion for what you do. You don't want to blow your own horn, and you know hard work should be rewarded. But the sad reality is that hard work often isn't enough, especially if no one sees you.

Visibility is one of the reasons people are promoted and given career-building roles. It's not the only reason, but it's a powerful one. And the good news is that your visibility is something you can magnify.

BEFORE YOU KICK OFF YOUR VISIBILITY PLAN

There's one major prerequisite you need to check before launching a visibility strategy. You need to make sure you're delivering what you've been asked to deliver. If you're not performing as expected—or better—all the visibility in the world won't help you get where you want to be. In David's case, he had clear feedback from his previous performance appraisals and 360-degree feedback. He knew how he was viewed by others.

Just as you shouldn't try a new exercise program or a diet without your doctor's approval, you need to get a clean bill of health in terms of your performance before you start. To achieve this, you can take one or all of these approaches:

- Check your previous performance reviews. Is there anything you need to work on before moving on?
- If it's been a long time since your last performance review, ask your manager for feedback.
- See if you are eligible to get 360-degree feedback and get it from a mix of people you work with, not just the friendly ones.

You'll want to look for feedback on whether you're getting the job done and how effectively you're doing it. Look for anything about your style and behaviors that might need to be addressed. If there's something you need to work on, embrace it and work on it. You can work on your own or ask for help from your manager, a colleague, or a coach.

Sometimes, you aren't in a position to deliver outcomes, but you're already in a highly visible situation. That's a pressure-filled position I once found myself in.

I'd just been asked by the consulting firm I worked for to start up an organizational development (OD) practice. The concept of OD was still very new, and my firm had no experience and no reputation in the area, which is probably why they asked me—a new employee with a recent MBA—to build it from scratch. I came up with a basic strategy that the partners approved.

However, even before I assembled a new team and developed our client services and product offerings, partners would walk past my office and ask, "Do you have any clients yet?" Of course, they asked that question! I had hired consultants and was using the firm's resources, with no clients in sight. They were nervous. Clearly, without revenue, I wasn't delivering. But how could I, being only weeks in the role? I decided to redefine delivery in this situation.

I put together a one-page report that showed the actions my team had taken in the past week, potential clients we'd contacted, proposals we'd sent out, and the expected revenue outcomes (what we expected to bill times our estimate of the probability that we would get the work). With this simple report, I could project the income we would earn by the end of the financial year.

I updated and sent this report to the partners on a weekly basis, calmed their fears, and stopped the questions. This provided a substitute for delivery until we could actually deliver, which started to happen within a few months.

WAYS TO BECOME MORE VISIBLE

Once you have delivery covered, you can start exploring ways to increase your visibility and create a visibility plan.

Your visibility plan will be unique to you. There are many visibility tactics, suited to different types of individuals. Some will be more appropriate for extroverts; others will be better for introverts. You can choose what will work for your temperament and talents.

Eleven suggestions to enhance your visibility, starting now

Look at the suggestions below and pick one or two that appeal to you.

Visibility Enhancer 1: Speak up in meetings.

What can you do if you hesitate to speak up in meetings? In some cases, your hesitation may reflect shyness, introversion, or a lack of confidence. Or you may be jaded by meeting dominators who talk non-stop and leave no space for others, even when they have nothing new to add.

When participating in large meetings, you must speak up promptly to avoid missing the opportunity. Marian, a mid-level, brilliant, and deeply thoughtful manager in a large global organization, likened it to Double-Dutch jump rope. (You may remember the game from elementary school—a game with two jump ropes crisscrossing at the same time.) You must pick the right moment, jump in, and commit fully. Regardless of your reasons for hesitation, it's essential to speak up and be heard.

Some tips to ramp up your contribution:

- **Create space to prepare.** Workdays can get packed with back-to-back meetings, and sometimes, you may not even know the topic or the purpose of the meeting you just dialed in to. This makes it less likely that you'll participate. You're probably focused on figuring out what's going on—and hoping others don't realize you're playing catch-up. Try to create space between your meetings, and if you can't do that, you may be able to prepare first thing in the morning before the day starts. Even five minutes of preparation will help you to be an active participant.
- **Know what point(s) you want to make.** As you prepare, write down at least one point you want to make, and keep it with you. You can visualize yourself saying

it, practice it out loud, or read it just before the meeting. You'll be much more likely to make that point if you take a moment to do this.

- **Make your point early in the meeting.** If you speak up early, you'll often find you've broken the silence barrier. When people respond to what you've said, it makes it easier to speak up again.
- **Get on the agenda.** In many organizations, someone sends out the agendas in advance and asks for input. Make sure you read and respond to this request, considering suggestions that could be useful and how you can contribute.
- **Agree with someone out loud.** If someone else makes a point that you agree with, say so, and say why. You can do it in a few words. It can be as simple as, "I agree; that's been my experience with frustrated customers, as well." If appropriate, build on that point. People need to know they've been heard, that their views are supported, and that their work colleagues are with them. Messages can get overlooked if someone doesn't agree out loud.

I remember one leadership meeting when one of the participants made a bold point. No one said anything, positive or negative, about the point she'd made, and the meeting moved on. She later told me how isolated and embarrassed she felt that her comment wasn't acknowledged, and she said this wasn't the first time this had happened. To her, it felt like her ideas weren't valued. She told me that she was looking for another job. That's how much she needed to be heard.

Visibility Enhancer 2: Get involved with stakeholders.

Consider your team's stakeholders—not just those you encounter daily, but also those in other parts of your organization. Often, these are people you haven't taken the time to connect with. You can offer to attend their team meetings to get to know their goals and issues better, or you can invite a stakeholder to present to your team.

Listening to stakeholders has a triple-powered effect of increasing your knowledge, connections, and visibility at the same time.

You'll learn more about the power of stakeholders and the importance of great stakeholder relationships in Strategy 5, and again in Strategy 7.

Visibility Enhancer 3: Speak in front of groups.

If you're up for this, speaking is one of the best ways to increase your visibility. Develop and create a presentation about your area of expertise or an area of interest. TED talks have shown us that short presentations can be powerful, and that the best ones often don't need slides. Slides run the risk of death by bullet point. If you have a gift for great slides, by all means use them; otherwise, you might do something else creative. Use props or engage your audience with stories. Personally, I don't like giving presentations. However, I enjoy running interactive workshops, so I often change my presentations into mini-workshops. It works well for me and serves to change audiences into participants, which aids learning and increases satisfaction.

Visibility Enhancer 4: Participate in expert panels.

Sometimes, an opportunity will come up for you to be on a panel, but you may hesitate because you don't feel like an expert. Maybe you're not quite up to the level of the erudite scholars on the panel, but you can do some research, find your perspective, have a point of view, and go for it. In fact, when you're on a panel, the expert approach can be dull, even mind-numbing. Remember those boring panels you've attended at conferences? Often, those highly qualified people go on and on and leave audience members with their eyes glazed over. The expert approach can lack humor, practical examples, spontaneity, and connection. Here are two ways you can be better on a panel or in any speaking situation:

- *Be yourself.* Frances Frei is a Harvard Business School professor who specializes in trust. In fact, her work challenge was to rebuild trust with Uber at a time when public trust for the business was at an all-time low. Frei says in her TED talk, "We, as a human species, can sniff out in a moment (literally in a moment) whether or not someone is being their authentic true self. So, in many ways, the prescription is clear. You don't want to have an authenticity wobble? Be you."
- *Focus on your audience.* What do they need to hear? What will help them grow? Will it help them feel validated? Acknowledge the expertise in the whole room, not just on the panel. Leave everyone with something they can take back to the office or home.

Visibility Enhancer 5: Write articles.

You can magnify what you know by writing articles that get published in your industry's journals. Local newspapers and magazines are another option. Or you can post articles within your organization's social media or newsletters. Articles are a useful way to create long-term visibility because people can save them, distribute them, and quote them for months—or years—to come.

Visibility Enhancer 6: Use LinkedIn.

LinkedIn is currently the most important social media business connector between people who work in organizations, whether for-profit or nonprofit. Even if you don't enjoy social media, if you work in business, you need a profile—the best profile you can come up with. LinkedIn provides guidelines as you build your profile, or you can find books and articles on the topic, or use AI to help you optimize your profile. So, make sure you have a LinkedIn presence. LinkedIn provides opportunities to connect with others, share points of view, and learn about career changes for people you've worked with in the past.

A client recently prepared for a job interview for an internal position in her organization. She showed me the tips she'd been given from her company, which included a suggestion to review the hiring manager's (and other interviewers') LinkedIn profiles in advance to get to know something about them. This enabled her to find relevant points to make and relevant questions to ask, which was great advice.

Also, keep in mind that the interviewer will almost certainly review your LinkedIn profile, which can expand your resume in powerful ways. Recruiters tell us that resumes in the US should be limited to one or two pages, but there are no such restrictions for your LinkedIn profile. Does your profile tell a great story about you? Don't just make it an online resume; include all that might be of interest. This will bring additional color and context to your profile.

You can also use LinkedIn to publish articles, share video presentations, connect with others you wouldn't normally get to know, and let people know if you are on the job market, which LinkedIn allows you to do privately or publicly. You can also ask people to write recommendations for you, which can be an invaluable testament to the value you bring.

Visibility Enhancer 7: Use your in-house social media platform.

If your company is large, it may have a strong in-house platform for internal announcements and employee sharing. You can apply many of the same LinkedIn ideas to these platforms: articles, team successes, and connecting with people outside of your immediate business area.

Visibility Enhancer 8: Teach what you know.

A great way to increase your visibility is to teach whatever you specialize in. Your company may give you the opportunity to speak at in-house forums or run webinars. Or you can do this with an industry association or potentially through a university. University professors often look for people who can come in and speak on a real-world application of their subject. Don't wait for someone to reach out to you; look for a university in your area and find out which ones have classes in which you could contribute.

Visibility Enhancer 9: Create events, large or small.

Events can provide great ways to support what you want to stand for at work in an authentic and powerful way and to publicly show leadership. You can create small, informal events like brainstorming sessions, meetings of like-minded people, or social events, or you can invest your time in creating a large, impactful event.

- *Small event approach:* Margot, in her sixties, was at the peak of her career, working on high-profile coaching assignments. She brought together a small roundtable of independent consultants and coaches she knew and respected—all people who worked to make a positive impact on the community. They met monthly and shared what they were working on, tapping into each other's ideas and wisdom. Over time, they began working together on meaningful projects. There was no cost to bringing these people together and no expectation about results. It was just a time to connect and explore how they could support each other.
- *Large event approach:* Here's one that has been close to my heart. As a chapter leader for a global business organization called Conscious Capitalism, I was part

of a team that put together conferences to help explore how business could be a force for good in the world. We identified local business founders and leaders who spoke at these conferences about their business's higher purpose and how they brought it to life. Over time, our work brought these ideas to thousands of people.

It took considerable time and effort on a volunteer basis, but these large events were deeply satisfying, aligned with my values and passions, and had a side benefit of increasing my visibility as I took on roles, such as master of ceremonies, panel moderator, host, or opening or closing the event.

Admittedly, large events like these are a lot of work, but if it's a cause you care about, it will likely be worth it.

Visibility Enhancer 10: Take on a leadership role in an employee resource group (ERG).

Many sizable companies have ERGs. (Your company may use a different name.) These are groups that come together to create connections, celebrate, and foster the development of specific segments of the population common to your workplace. Examples of these are:

- Women's networks
- Veterans' networks
- Networks for BIPOC employees (these may be split into specific networks for each group)

- Networks for international employees
- LGBTQIA+ networks
- Networks for people with disabilities
- Mental health advocacy networks
- Young professionals' networks
- Older workers networks

These groups often will give you an opportunity to meet others from across the business, and they usually welcome people who are prepared to take some sort of leadership or support role.

You'll meet interesting people and may have access to senior leaders who participate as sponsors for the ERGs.

Visibility Enhancer 11: Write a paper on an issue that needs to change in your business, then share it with the right people.

This is a great initiative if you're a good writer and can do the research to back up your idea. The paper shouldn't be long, maybe one page front and back. The people you want to read it tend to be very busy, so get to the point quickly, but still make sure you have strong data and a couple of stories to back it up. Here's one of my favorite examples:

Debra was a mid-level leader in her thirties, originally from Australia, whose US career took off quickly. She earned a prestigious MBA, then joined a reputable consulting firm for a few years and was recruited from there to lead a division in a global financial advisory firm. After a successful stint there, she and her husband moved back to Sydney with their two young children. To spend time with her children before they started school, Debra wanted to work a four-day week, but she didn't see that as something that should hold her career growth back.

Alas, a request for a four-day workweek was all it took to make Debra become invisible. In those days—the early 2000s—most big corporations didn't understand that there could be a different way to work and that they needed to adapt their approach to attract talent, such as women like Debra.

It might not have helped that Debra looked younger than her age, that she had natural humility, and that she showed warmth when she talked to others. (Note: research has shown that women are sometimes stereotyped as one of two extremes: "warm and incompetent" or "cold and competent," which can put them in a double bind.) Her best offer was with an Australian wealth firm in a position two levels lower than her previous role in an area that was out of the limelight.

She knew she needed to polish her brand and increase her visibility, so we set to work exploring what she wanted to stand for in the workplace. We looked at important ways she could demonstrate her many strengths (strategy and marketing were huge areas of expertise), but in the end, she remembered her frustration with the way her business treated women employees with an almost complete lack of opportunities for part-time work, job-sharing, or flexible work practices. The traditional view was that these practices weren't appropriate at leadership levels, and people who asked for flexibility showed a lack of commitment to the job.

She knew that research showed that businesses were much more successful when they had women on the executive team and on their boards. But hiring managers and even HR departments seemed to doubt that flexible work practices could present a viable route to success. Women had to adapt to the traditional way men had worked throughout the history of corporations: full-time work in the office and networking through golf, sporting events, and the occasional dinner or drinks out.

Repeatedly, Debra would return to how the business missed out on valuable talent and experience by its failure to adapt to the needs of senior working women, and she'd shake her head with frustration, asking, "Why can't they see it?"

This was her burning passion at this time, a problem she understood in a way that apparently no one else did. She clearly saw that her company needed to design work in a new way that acknowledged the needs of working parents and their families and thereby attract talented working mothers to roles at all levels. She knew this approach would be a win-win. This was what she wanted to see changed, so she designed a plan to change it. She decided to write a paper.

She pulled together the relevant data and global case studies, then kept it real by interviewing two groups of women:

- *Tenured women who'd made it to senior levels in her organization: Debra talked to them about how they thought their career paths had differed from those of their male counterparts, and she asked them what they had to give up along the way.*
- *Younger women starting out in their careers at her company: Debra interviewed them about their expectations regarding work and family, and how they might want the firm to adapt its policies to enable them to perform at their best.*

The very first female senior-level executive she interviewed was impressed by her knowledge and research, and she told Debra that part of the organization's vision (which had not yet been communicated) was to become an employer of choice for women. A committee of executives had already been formed. When she heard Debra's explanation of the issues and the research approach she was taking, the executive invited Debra to become part of that committee.

They listened to and valued her research and decided to send her to Harvard for a residential program on women in leadership, then share what she learned with every division in her firm.

No longer invisible, Debra found herself overwhelmed with job offers, ranging from strategy to operational leadership. She continued to grow and is now the CEO of a large financial advisory firm.

She's not only successful but also publicly committed to the best work practices that will attract a diverse workforce at every level. The company she leads has grown, and they consistently win awards for their family-friendly practices and their contributions to the community.

There are a lot of ideas above for you to ponder—so many ways to be visible! You don't need to try them all. Consider which ones will provide the easiest jumping-off point for your increased visibility, based on what you want to stand for and your values and strengths.

Finally, remember David from the beginning of this chapter, who missed out on the big job he wanted and was about to walk out the door? He didn't quit after all. Once he realized that visibility was a key component of success, he adopted the idea of a visibility strategy with enthusiasm.

He used many of the visibility enhancers above to help him to get noticed by the people who hadn't seen him before. Only a few months after we started our work together, he got the first of many promotions. Soon, he became one of those people everybody knew. Within a few years, he was on the executive potential list, and he ultimately made it to the C-Suite, where he led the bank's largest division.

RISE WITH COURAGE

"The best protection any woman can have. . . is courage."

—Elizabeth Cady Stanton

A WORKPLACE IS A community, like any other. As a community, it gives you a place to belong for eight (give or take) hours a day. That can come with good parts, like connection, achievement, reward, enjoyment, and fulfilment, and it can also come with hard parts, like disappointment, conflict, insecurity, overwork, and even failure. At the beginning, everything seems bright and shiny, but reality eventually sets in. Do any of these comments sound familiar? "Now that I'm a month in, my job is not what I was told it would be," or "The people I work with aren't friendly or collaborative," or "I don't have the time or resources to do what's being asked of me."

One quality that separates the successful from the unsuccessful is how they face the hard parts. There are always hard parts. They help you become a better leader. You have a few choices when facing something hard or unpleasant at work:

1. **You can suffer through it** for as long as you work in the organization and miss the opportunities to grow and learn the valuable lessons that come from challenges.
2. **You can run from it** by finding a new job (which you'll soon learn has its own set of problems).
3. **You can face it** with courage.

How you face the hard things is the measure of whether you'll succeed long-term. Courage is a key differentiator for success.

There are three kinds of courage that will change your life at work or anywhere: the courage to step up, the courage to open up, and the courage to speak up.

When you step up, you stretch yourself and do what needs to be done when it needs to be done—even when it's hard.

> HOW YOU FACE THE HARD THINGS IS THE MEASURE OF WHETHER YOU'LL SUCCEED LONG-TERM. COURAGE IS A KEY DIFFERENTIATOR FOR SUCCESS.

When you step up, you put up your hand to take responsibility. When you step up, you do hard things, often things you didn't realize you knew how to do. Women are usually good at stepping up if they are asked to. If tapped on the shoulder, women are willing to take on the seemingly unsolvable problems and take on the extra team or project. However, women are also less likely than men to put themselves forward for those same assignments and less likely to promote themselves as being capable.

> THERE ARE THREE KINDS OF COURAGE THAT WILL CHANGE YOUR LIFE AT WORK OR ANYWHERE: THE COURAGE TO STEP UP, THE COURAGE TO OPEN UP, AND THE COURAGE TO SPEAK UP.

When you open up, you bring yourself fully to work. You're authentic, vulnerable, and show your imperfections. Women can be very good at being real. We're often warm, personable, and willing to talk about life, values, and interests. We rarely go into supercompetitive mode (you know, the "pissing contests" some competitive men embrace).

When you speak up, you say what needs to be said, especially when no one else takes the lead. You notice when something is wrong, and you call it. You have the conversations others avoid. You stand up for what is right, and you advocate—sometimes for others, sometimes for yourself. You ask good questions, and you ask for help when you need it.

It is here that women often struggle: they often hesitate to say the hard thing that needs to be said. They may bottle it up and feel like they're going to burst, vent with friends, or suffer in silence. The women I work with often say, "I don't know; I just don't like confrontation, and I'm not good at it."

So, it's time to talk about:

- Why it's so hard to have courageous conversations
- Why it's critical to have them
- The essential stages of a courageous conversation
- How to prepare yourself to have them
- How to position yourself to listen to the other person
- How to get the outcomes you need (which is not necessarily the same thing as winning)

If you learn to develop the muscle to have these conversations, it will pay you back throughout your career and your life.

How do you develop physical muscle when lifting weights? You use the muscle more and in a different way than you normally use it, creating tiny tears that, after recovery, make it stronger than it was before. Anyone who has developed muscle will tell you it's not an easy process. It takes work and dedication, and at times, it feels impossible. But if you do it repeatedly, you'll start to see that change, that definition. You'll be stronger. The muscle of courage is the same.

Let's look at a real-life example of someone who developed her muscle to speak up:

Julia, an operations manager, had just completed a workshop on how to have courageous conversations. Back in the office after the session, she was called out of a meeting by her 2 ½ -year-old son's preschool teacher, who told her that her normally quiet and happy son had cried nonstop for an hour. They couldn't figure out what was wrong. The teacher thought he might be ill and asked Julia to come pick him up.

Julia did what so many working mothers have done. She left the meeting to pick up her son. As she walked up the pre-school steps, she could hear his distressed wailing. Worried, she called his pediatrician, who was (miraculously) able to see him on short notice.

When the doctor checked him, Julia was shocked to learn that his arm was fractured. Julia and the doctor asked her son questions. Through his tears, he managed to communicate that another child had jumped on him while he was playing.

Julia was furious. Not only had this happened in preschool, but no one had seen it happen. On the drive home, her son's small arm in a cast, she thought about what she should do. Go back and give them a piece of her mind? Tell other parents? Take him out of the preschool immediately? As angry as she was, she hesitated to go to battle with the preschool staff. There had to be a better way.

After she got him home and settled him down for a nap, she thought about our workshop on the principles of courageous conversations and considered how she should respond.

WE ALL NEED COURAGE TO SPEAK UP

There are conversations we all need to have on occasion—at work or at home—that are simply hard. And as necessary as they are, most of us tend to avoid them as long as we possibly can.

So, how do you have conversations that you know are going to be really, really uncomfortable?

This is one of the most frequent issues for my clients, especially my female clients. While I want to support them, the truth is that I am a former confrontation wimp. Early in my career as a coach, this was a drawback, since a big part of my job involved giving people feedback—often feedback they didn't want to hear.

So, many years ago, I made it my business to understand how confrontation works and what makes it go wrong. I decided to work on my confrontation skills, attending workshops and reading every book I could find on the topic. And I learned from people who already did this very well. Soon, I noticed my confrontations became more effective. And I was more confident when I had to have them.

As I learned how to navigate the stormy waters of conflict and shared what I'd learned with my clients, they found the same greatly improved outcomes. In their feedback, they often cited these ideas as the most valuable part of their coaching programs.

Yes, women seem to be more conflict-averse than their male colleagues. That doesn't mean that men are better at conflict; they're simply more prepared to have it, whether or not they have the skills to do it well.

However, women, who've often been raised to care and be supportive, can be great at confronting others once they've learned a few skills. That's what we'll work on here.

But first, I'd like to ask you to identify a courageous conversation you need to have or one you had recently that didn't go well. It will help to have a specific conversation in mind as you go through this chapter.

What courageous conversation do you need to have? Maybe it's with:

- The manager who blithely accepted praise for an idea that was yours
- The team member who comes unprepared for meetings
- The colleague who undermines you behind your back

- The customer who had a foul-mouthed outburst with a member of your team

Those are work examples, but it can be just as hard to have these conversations in our personal lives. Your partner is late everywhere you go. Your neighbor has a constantly yapping dog. Your in-laws feed your children sugar-filled treats and then tell them not to tell you, and on and on. You know you need to talk to them, but when you imagine that conversation, your heart sinks, your stomach clenches, and your throat tightens.

EVERYONE NEEDS THE SKILLS TO INITIATE AND HAVE HARD CONVERSATIONS.

So, you don't do it.

Or maybe you do have the conversation, but it's awkward; you don't do it well, and it backfires.

Everyone needs the skills to initiate and have hard conversations. Developing these skills is worth the effort, as you'll soon see. The good news is that these skills can be learned. And with every conversation you have, you'll develop that muscle and will get better at it over time.

WHY IS THIS SO IMPORTANT?

There are many reasons you need to have hard conversations. These are three of the most important:

1. **It's the right thing to do.** You may not have thought of this as an issue of integrity, but avoiding the

conversation is a form of dishonesty that puts you and others in a bad situation.

2. **It's your job.** If you're a leader or aspire to become one, this is an essential part of your role.

3. **You'll be more successful.** You'll stand out as a much more effective leader because of this skill.

Let's explore each of these a little more.

1. It's the right thing to do.

As a ten-year-old, when I came home from school, my stay-at-home mother would often be engrossed in afternoon soap operas while she ironed my father's shirts. Like so many other women of her generation, she used the soaps for both entertainment and life lessons. One of her observations was that the characters constantly told small and big lies to avoid confrontation. In her view, if they had just told the truth from the start, there would be no story, no next episode.

At a doctor's office recently, the TV in the waiting room showed that even with the newer soaps, nothing has changed. The lies and the drama are still there, hooking new audiences.

It would be easy to say that these lies were written for entertainment purposes only, but the characters are often surprisingly true-to-life. They avoid confrontation for the same reasons you and I are tempted to. In the short run, it makes things easier. However, in the long run, if you avoid the truth, even in small ways, you can experience serious and damaging effects for yourself and others. Trust may be broken, serious issues may be hidden, and people may be hurt.

Angela, an ambitious, bright young professional, confided in me after a workshop, "My work makes me miserable. My manager gives the same two people all the good assignments, and the rest of us are left with grunt work. Everyone is so discouraged. We're all just going through the motions. It's not getting any better, and I've decided to look for another job."

"Have you talked to your manager about this? Have you asked for feedback or told him you'd like some better assignments?" I asked.

"No," she said, tears welling in her eyes. "I don't want to get branded as a complainer. It would just make things worse. It's better for me to just leave."

Perhaps something similar has happened to you. A problem is obvious to you and everyone else, but your manager is either oblivious or, worse, perhaps it's intentional. Which are you more likely to do? Stay quiet and find another job? Or talk to your manager, lay out the situation, and share the impact it has on you and your colleagues?

Let's be honest. Because of the dread of that conversation, many people, perhaps especially women who learned the importance of harmony as young girls, would be more likely to find another job and quietly leave without explanation. Maybe you've done it in a previous role. I know I did it at least once early in my career.

However, is it the right thing to do? In most cases, probably not. Your manager needs to be aware that the problem exists and how it is impacting you and others. They need to have a chance to fix it, and they need to know the consequences if they don't. You may rationalize your actions and say to yourself, "Surely my manager must know," but there's a good chance that they don't know or at least don't understand it with the clarity you have. They need the perspective you can bring. They need the nudge of awareness you can give.

Finally, if you don't speak up, you don't only let yourself and your manager down, but you also let your colleagues down. They are left with the mess that drove you to leave. Some of them may not be in a position to leave a secure job. So, they'll continue to struggle in the toxic muck you managed to escape.

That's exactly what Angela did in this case. She posted her new job on LinkedIn and told me how relieved she was to have found a new opportunity. She didn't learn or grow from taking on the challenge of talking to her boss, and I'd be willing to bet that the next time she needs to have a difficult conversation with her new manager, she won't do it.

2. It's your job.

Too often, I see managers with under-performers who won't have hard conversations with those people. Just recently, I spoke with a partner in a law firm who breathed a sigh of relief as she handed off a poor performer to another part of the firm. True, she thought that person might be more successful in the other practice area, so she felt it could be a win-win. Maybe it was.

However, she still needed to have a conversation with the person who was struggling. That person moved on in quiet desperation, unaware of exactly what went wrong. A huge growth opportunity was missed for both of them.

As the leader, it's your job to have that conversation. You need to tell them what you see, share the facts, explain why it can't continue, work through what needs to change, and offer your help and support. It's your job to give poor performers feedback. It's their responsibility to decide whether they will act on it. Then, it's your responsibility to take action if they don't or can't. That's part of what you're there to do.

3. You'll be more successful.

In one of my favorite books, *Crucial Conversations: Tools for Talking when the Stakes are High*, the authors share how they came to realize the critical importance of this skill. They (a team of consultants) had been hired to identify the skills and abilities needed for leadership success in an organization, and they interviewed the most highly rated leaders. By shadowing these leaders through their day-to-day meetings and tasks, they saw that many of the leaders had similar capabilities. However, one specific skill sets the best leaders apart: the ability to have effective conversations in difficult situations. The ability to speak truth to power. The ability to give feedback that could be hard for the other person to hear but was exactly what they needed to hear.

The person who's courageous and deals proactively with issues with clarity, calmness, and care, will—in the long term—be more successful than the person who doesn't.

HOW TO DECIDE IF YOU NEED TO HAVE A COURAGEOUS CONVERSATION

Does every situation have to turn into a courageous conversation? Here are some questions you can ask yourself to help you decide:

What will happen if I don't have the conversation? Is it likely to get better on its own?

Some situations do. But many, many do not.

> *When I was an entry-level consultant in a large consulting firm, I asked a more experienced colleague for help with a client problem. The client had openly expressed dissatisfaction with some work we had done. My colleague looked at me with a weary smile and said, "I find that if I leave things alone, they eventually sort themselves out."*
>
> *Wow! I thought. Maybe I shouldn't take client complaints to heart quite so much. Maybe they will just sort themselves out. Within months, my colleague suddenly disappeared from the firm without explanation. And, while I never knew for certain, I suspected that his "leave it alone and hope it will get better" attitude was a part of the reason why he was gone.*

Think about this: if it's truly a hard conversation, it probably won't get better on its own.

Could the conversation make things worse in our relationship?

This is what most of us fear—that a frank, honest conversation will backfire on us. We're afraid we'll make an already shaky relationship worse.

The skills in this chapter will help you to have these conversations without the mistakes that could make things worse, such as if you:

- Fail to give any context for the conversation.
- Don't get the other person's agreement to have the conversation: you talk *at* them instead of *with* them.

- Dump on them—you let your anger, resentment, or irritation get in the way of fair and honest communication.
- Tell them the way you see the situation but don't ask how they see it.
- Insist on a single outcome rather than exploring other ways to resolve the issue.

These are common mistakes many of us commit when we deal with conflict. Below, we'll learn a better way. When you use these principles, your relationship with the other person is likely to be strengthened.

THE FIVE PARTS OF A COURAGEOUS CONVERSATION

When you have a courageous conversation, there are five parts you need to approach with consciousness and insight. You need to:

1. Prepare yourself to have the conversation.
2. Prepare to hear the other person.
3. Set up the conversation for success.
4. Have the conversation.
5. Agree on next actions and follow-through.

Let's explore each of these.

Part 1: Prepare yourself to have the conversation.

Preparing yourself doesn't usually take a lot of time, but it will make so much difference when you find yourself in the middle of the conversation.

There are two aspects of personal preparation—the facts (and your story around them) and your intent. First, you need to get your facts together. To do this, you must be able to tell the difference between a fact and an opinion.

The facts

A fact is observable. Gervase Bush, in his book *Clear Leadership*, likens a fact to the image and sounds captured in an unaltered, unedited video. You can hear what was said. It's indisputable. You can see what happened. No one can argue with it. That's what makes facts so powerful—all parties agree on them.

An opinion is how you've made sense of the facts.

"My colleague argued against a proposal he'd told me privately that he supported" might be a fact.

"My colleague can't be trusted" is an opinion. It's how you made sense of that.

Both facts and opinions are important. Facts are something you both agree upon, but people can come up with wildly different stories about what those facts mean. It's important to recognize that you have created a story around the facts. And it's just that—a story. It's not the absolute truth, no matter how good you think your story is.

Have you ever had an experience when someone else completely misunderstood something you said or did? They made a whole story around it that wasn't at all what you intended. Communication is hard, and we misread, misinterpret, and misunderstand each other every single day. We take a few data points, and we draw a conclusion that may or may not be right. We guess. We speculate. We insist. We do everything except ask.

"Look at it from his perspective," your well-meaning colleagues say to you. So, you do, and you're proud of yourself for being open-minded.

That's a good start, but it's still a guess. It's still speculation. You still haven't asked. But that's all you have available to work with until you have the conversation. So, get your facts together (if possible, make sure you have them right), acknowledge that you've made up a story about those facts, and realize that the other person has made up their own story. Yours might be true.

COMMUNICATION IS HARD, AND WE MISREAD, MISINTERPRET, AND MISUNDERSTAND EACH OTHER EVERY SINGLE DAY. WE TAKE A FEW DATA POINTS, AND WE DRAW A CONCLUSION THAT MAY OR MAY NOT BE RIGHT.

Theirs might be true. More likely, it's something in between. Or it could be something you haven't even thought of. The truth is funny like that.

Clean intent

To have a productive conversation, it's critical to get your intent right. So, ask the question, "What's my intent for this conversation? Can I state it clearly? Is it clean? Almost every tough conversation at work will be improved if you stop to clarify and clean up your intent.

The purpose of this conversation may be to "create a path forward for how we work together." But a statement of intent like, "I want to find a way to work more collaboratively with you," takes it to another level. It makes it personal. It is an opener to a conversation that will help the other person hear what you have to say. You need to state your intent, and they need to hear it and decide if they believe you. Every statement of intent will be different, and it's important to think it through with your head and your heart.

If your coworker seems determined to butt heads with you, the intent for the conversation might be expressed as, "We've had some conflict over time and haven't worked together well. My intent for this meeting is for us to find a way to fix this and create a path forward that's respectful and harmonious. I'd like to share what I see going wrong, but I know that's just my perspective. I want to hear what your experience has been. And I want to come out of this with shared understanding and a plan for a better way."

Notice that there is no anger, resentment, or blame in this statement. That's because you've created a statement that shows clean intent. The easiest way to understand clean intent is to first look at what it isn't.

It's not clean intent if:

- You aim to railroad the other person into a predetermined outcome.
- You're angry with them and want to vent that anger.
- You'd like to embarrass them, humiliate them, or get revenge.
- You have no interest in their point of view.

If you realize that you're about to have a conversation without clean intent, don't have the conversation yet. Put it on hold until tomorrow, and then this evening, focus on cleaning up your intent.

At this point, if you're like most of us, you may realize that there have been times you haven't operated with clean intent. You're not alone. We all have the experience of being angry or vindictive. We've all communicated in harmful ways, perhaps even for much of our lives. We learned it in the schoolyard, on social media, or maybe even in the way our families interacted with each other. We see plenty of evidence of this with extended family at holiday gatherings. But with this new awareness, you can shift that. With this one change, you can improve your communication from this point forward.

"But wait," I hear you say, "won't I make myself vulnerable to others if I don't play by the same 'gotcha' rules they play with?" While that might seem to make sense, you'll usually find that clean intent is contagious. It disarms. It stops others in their tracks. The intent changes everything, as in the conversation below.

Neville and Shona, mid-level leaders in a competitive global tech company, had a longstanding feud. They actively disliked each other, and neither one seemed motivated to fix the situation. Both were young, up-and-coming leaders. Both were ambitious and saw each other as competitors for the limited senior positions at the next level.

Shona had been raised in Ireland and was very close to her father, a brilliant playwright and professor who was her role model in life. When her father passed away suddenly, she flew home for his funeral but had to return shortly afterward because she was in the middle of a major project with a tight deadline.

Neville had lost his beloved mother two years earlier. He watched Shona's tired, pale face and downward gaze during meetings, and all his antipathy left him. He could see her grief and feel her pain. All he wanted to do was help. But when he tried to speak with her, she stiffened. Finally, he caught her when no one was around. He said, "I need to tell you something. My mother died recently, but I never talked about it at work, and I should have. I have a pretty good idea what you're going through. I went to a grief counselor, and she gave me a list of things to do that really helped me. I'd like to share the list with you if you want it. And I want you to know that I'm here for you if you need to talk about it."

After that, everything changed, and Neville and Shona became close colleagues who supported each other as their careers developed and grew. Neither had a bad word to say about the other ever again.

Tips to find clean intent

It's surprisingly easy to figure out if your intent is clean. People somehow just intuitively get it. When asked, they usually know what's in the way. Most of them also know what they need to do to make it clean. I think you will, too.

Here are some principles to bear in mind:

- Recognize that holding on to past anger, resentment, or other negative emotions won't get you anywhere. It's time to let go. Holding on to those emotions hurts only you.
- If you find it hard to clean up your intent, you can ask a wise friend, colleague, or coach to help you set aside those negative emotions. They may be able to help you see the right thing to do in this situation.
- Create a succinct written statement of your intent. If you write your intent, you will be more likely to feel it and internalize it.
- Practice stating your intent out loud, either in the mirror or in front of someone you trust. This helps you to check to see if your nonverbal behavior is in alignment with your statement. If your words say one thing, but your eyes, gestures, and tone say something else, you need to do more work.

Here's the magic: if your intent is clean, you'll be able to say whatever needs to be said to anyone who needs to hear it. It will liberate you in future conversations with your colleagues, managers, neighbors, in-laws, or your teenager.

Part 2: Prepare to hear the other person.

I first learned the power of listening many years ago when I was hired to work with a company that baked cookies and crackers in Australia. New legislation around equal employment opportunity for women had been passed, and I was called in to help this food manufacturing business update its practices in light of the new law.

It didn't take long for me to see that they had a problem. The bulk of their workforce was neatly divided into two groups: bakers and packers. The bakers combined the ingredients and baked them in powerful, huge ovens. The packers took the finished products and packed them so they could be distributed to supermarkets.

The problem was that the bakers had always been an all-male workforce, and the packers had always been all-female, mostly women who'd immigrated to Australia from several different countries. Maybe that alone wouldn't have been such a problem, but bakers were paid twice as much as packers.

The general manager of the factory asked me to explain the legislation and the company's need to comply with it to the team leaders and union delegates. But first, I had to meet with the bakehouse manager, who oversaw the operations for both bakers and packers.

The bakehouse manager wore all white with a jaunty white baker's cap. He had a pink face and could have personally posed for the supermarket packages for the company's cookies. I confidently explained the new legislation to him and the problems I'd seen when I reviewed their pay structures.

Wow. No one had prepared me for his response. His jolly pink coloring took on a deeper, more dangerous magenta hue. He was furious. And I got the full force of his fury. He told me that there was no %^&* way they would be complying with this legislation, and he listed all the reasons why. Here's the gist of what he said:

In the baking area:

- The flour bags were too heavy for women.
- The machines broke down and had to be fixed.
- The temperature in the baking area was incredibly hot, and the women wouldn't be able to stand it.
- The language the men used would offend the women.

In the packing area:

- Many women didn't speak English. He said they'd made accommodations for this in the packing area, but they couldn't do the same in the baking area.
- Because of their cultural and religious backgrounds, he said that the women's husbands wouldn't allow them to work with men.
- The women, many of whom were neighbors or even related, enjoyed chatting with each other as they worked and would find it uncomfortable if men were present.

All of this was sprinkled with angry sarcasm and a sneer on his face. I'd never experienced so much direct animosity before, and honestly, I didn't know how to respond. On some level, I recognized this wasn't about me, but the message I brought was a clear threat to the way he'd always run his bakehouse, or even more importantly, it was a threat to his way of life.

So, I listened carefully, asked for clarification, took notes, and then summarized back to him what I had heard (without the expletives). I let him know that I could see that this was hard, and I could understand his concern. And I could.

I took a deep breath as I shut my red spiral notebook and asked two questions: "Is it possible that there are two or three women, current packers, who are strong enough and tough enough to work in the baker's section? And could there be one or two men who might fit into the packer's culture?"

I knew this wasn't much progress, but I hoped this might prepare us to take a baby step. There were many assertions he'd made that I could have argued, but I knew this wasn't the time. This was the time to listen to his frustration, anger, and personal experiences.

The next week, when I met with the team leaders and union delegates, I felt anxious. The bakehouse manager had ominously warned me that they would be a much tougher audience than he was. He said (in colorful Australian vernacular) that they would "tear strips off" me. And to add to that, I'd found out the day before that the general manager—his direct boss who'd been scheduled to introduce the sessions—wasn't available to do so. To my dismay, I learned that my jolly friend in white would do my introductions for both sessions.

However, when he stood up to introduce me, he seemed like a different person. He told them that he'd met with me, that he'd shared their concerns with me, and he told them I'd listened. He believed I understood the issues. As a result, while he still had doubts, he said, "This is the law, and we have always been good corporate citizens. We'll find a way."

I completed my presentation, answered questions, and knew that we would, indeed, find a way.

Learn how to truly listen

When you learned to communicate, chances are that you didn't learn how to listen well (almost none of us did). But if you stop to think about it, you'll realize how important listening is. You know how devastating it feels when others don't listen to you. Maybe you've even left a job because you weren't heard. And remember the pain when you were a teenager pleading to use the car just this once, but your parent turned a deaf ear to you?

Yet, despite knowing how important it is to listen, almost all of us struggle to listen effectively. Why is it so hard? The many reasons could fill a whole book. But let's pick the big one: we don't listen because we learned exactly the opposite—how to make our point, argue our point, and win our point. Much of the time, we only listen enough to respond.

Chances are, it was modeled to us as children by the adults in our lives. And it's become an increasing problem with social media, where many people are constantly aggrieved, YELL-ING at each other IN ALL CAPS. It's unbelievably easy not to listen to each other online. But when we listen well, it can make the difference between a positive, enjoyable relationship and a complete relationship breakdown.

Barry-Wehmiller is a $3 billion, high-growth company, often referred to by Simon Sinek in his book *Leaders Eat Last* for its unusual approach to people leadership. Here is Barry-Wehmiller's Manifesto, which gives you an idea of the focus of this company:

Everyone wants to do better. Trust them.
Leaders are everywhere. Find them.

People achieve good things, big and small, every day. Celebrate them.
Some people wish things were different. Listen to them.
Everybody matters. Show them.

I once worked as a facilitator with Barry-Wehmiller. The program I co-facilitated, called "Listen Like a Leader," is the core requirement for Barry-Wehmiller University's leadership development. The premise is that you must, first and foremost, learn to be a great listener before you can be a great leader. This meant a full two days of in-person, highly interactive training. Not many companies go down a path like that.

People who've attended the program sometimes share how listening has changed their lives. Some tell how it's healed a relationship with a colleague or a team member or saved a parent-child relationship that had been circling the drain. Most people assume that they know how to listen, but once they've attended this program, they realize that's not the case.

Below are two ideas from the program that may help you prepare to listen to the other person.

- You cannot motivate another person. You can only create an environment in which people will motivate themselves.
- All people are motivated, but they behave to meet their needs, not yours.

There's only one foolproof way to ensure you understand the motivations of the other person, and that way is to listen. Once you've done that, you have a chance of co-creating a win-win outcome.

Lina, a manager at one of Barry-Wehmiller's manufacturing plants in Europe, told me a story about a day spent with Emily, a leader who was initially angry and aggressive with her. At first, it triggered Lina's defenses, but as she noticed how she felt, she remembered what she'd learned in the program. She stopped, became fully present, and listened. That changed the whole inter-action. She learned about Emily and the problems she faced, and together, they came up with small changes she could make to support Emily in her job. They ended their time together with a deep and mutually respectful relationship, far from where they had started.

You can prepare to listen in these two ways:

- Get curious. What do you want to know? What do you need to know?
- Prepare yourself so you won't be triggered. The other person may make a statement that triggers you emo-tionally. Be prepared for that to happen. Don't prepare so you can come back with a response—you'll have your time to respond later—but so you can listen more deeply. How will you stay calm and continue listening?

Part 3: Set up the conversation for success.

One day, as I worked in the office of a client, I was stunned to see a leader I'd always respected give direct, harsh feedback to one of her young team members right in the middle of the room. Apparently, she'd been unable to find a private room and chose not to wait. I sat a few feet away (as did many oth-ers) and cringed in discomfort. It was an interaction we never should have heard. The young woman's embarrassment was obvious. Later, I imagined that embarrassment might turn to other emotions, like shame or anger. The conversation obviously affected her. In fact, it affected everyone who heard it.

Clearly, this conversation hadn't been set up the way it should have been.

Here are some success tips for setting up the conversation.

- **Find a private place.** As in the example above, it's critical to have the interaction in a private place to make the conversation feel safe enough for the other person to respond.
- **Have the conversation as soon as you reasonably can.** If you wait for a week or more after the triggering event, people (including you) may suffer in the meantime. Having the conversation quickly also helps you both remember the facts of the situation because they're fresh in your minds.
- **Give yourself enough time.** Neither of you should have to race off to another engagement halfway through or sit there worrying that you'll miss an important meeting.
- **Practice.** If you're worried about how it will go, it could be helpful to have someone you trust help you prepare and role-play.

Part 4: Have the conversation.

Once you've prepared yourself, considered how you will listen, and set up the best possible place, time, and environment, it's time to have the conversation. Here are three steps for the conversation.

A. Start with an authentic opening statement.
B. Ask the other person/people to respond—and listen to their response.
C. Explore possibilities together.

Here's more on each of these steps.

A. Start with an authentic opening statement.

A key to a productive two-way conversation is a good opening statement, which is the shortest part of the conversation. It's short but important. It's essential to get this right. If you don't, the other person may not be able to hear what you have to say.

Susan Scott, author of the *New York Times* bestseller *Fierce Conversations*, says that your opening statement should not be longer than sixty seconds. For most of us, sixty seconds sounds insanely short. Many of us (me included) spent the early part of our adult life with long, explanation-full, meandering opening statements.

In my case, I finally learned. Early in my career as a consultant in Australia, I worked with a Macquarie University colleague to conduct a series of workshops with business executives to explore "the future of work." Through a connection, I had the chance to meet with Daniel Petrie, then-CEO of Microsoft Australia, and managed to score a cup of coffee with him to discuss the project. The goal was to ask if he would allow approximately twenty of his senior leaders to participate in the two-hour workshop. Here's how it went:

We sat outdoors at a cafe at the Microsoft campus in Sydney, ordered our coffees, and exchanged a few pleasantries (nervous pleasantries on my part). I was prepared—possibly too prepared.

I'd put together a long list of reasons why Microsoft should participate. My coffee went cold as I spent the entire time covering that list, enumerating the benefits of being part of the research.

Finally, I stopped to catch my breath, and Daniel asked, "Could I give you some feedback?" I nervously nodded yes. He said, "Thirty seconds in, you had me ready to say yes. Then you kept talking, and I wondered if this was really a good idea. You needed to get to the point, and then let me ask questions. You almost lost me."

Fortunately, he agreed to send his executives to the workshop. And I learned a valuable lesson I've never forgotten: say what you need to say quickly, then invite a response and, most importantly, shut up.

Think again about the courageous conversation you need to have. It's time to create your opening statement. While Susan Scott says to limit it to one minute, I find that opening statements need to be slightly longer—say, ninety seconds to two minutes. A one-minute opening statement often feels abrupt, and your goal is to create safety.

Your opening statement will:

- Show your (clean) intent for the conversation.
- State the facts and your story around the facts.
- Own any part you played in the problem, with an apology, if appropriate.

Let's look at these a bit more closely, with examples of each of these.

Show your intent. You've made the effort to consider your intent and clean it up if needed. That's half the battle (and if you've done this, you'll know the word "battle" isn't exaggerated).

You now know what your intent is. Tell the other person. This makes such a difference. When you share your intent, you invite the person to accept it or perhaps even shape it further.

Here's an example:

My intent for this conversation is to understand why the employee engagement scores for our division are the lowest in the company.

Sometimes, you can further clarify by stating what is *not* your intent. This can be helpful in situations when you realize the other party doesn't trust you or thinks you're trying to damage them in some way.

My intent for this meeting is not for anyone to point fingers or get raked over the coals. We're a team, and we need to come together and be honest about our obstacles. Let's share ownership and fix this so we can get our people engaged and working together.

State the facts briefly, and share your story around the facts. Remember, the facts are objective and observable. The story is how you've made sense of the facts.

In the above scenario, the facts and story might look like this:

Some very strong people have left our organization in the past year. The engagement survey shows that people in this group are frustrated, and some are looking for other jobs. More than half say they wouldn't recommend the company. It seems like there is something going on here that we need to explore.

When you share the facts and your story around the facts, the other person is likely to feel defensive, although they may or may not show it. Be careful to avoid labels and judgments. Be tentative about your story. The conclusions you've drawn might not be correct or might not be the whole story. Stay open to their story, which you're about to hear, once the opening is done.

While you try to be appropriately tentative, don't be intentionally vague and underplay serious problems or issues. It is kinder in the long run to be clearer now.

Own any part you've played in the problem. Many people get stuck on this one. They don't want to accept any of the blame. But if you're vulnerable and share your part in creating the problem, people feel much safer acknowledging their part in it.

> BE CAREFUL TO AVOID LABELS AND JUDGMENTS... THE CONCLUSIONS YOU'VE DRAWN MIGHT NOT BE CORRECT OR MIGHT NOT BE THE WHOLE STORY.

You don't have to own the whole responsibility (or even 50 percent), but it's a good idea to share some responsibility if you can. When two people have an issue or problem, it is almost never only one person's fault. Stretch your memory. Was there something you could have done to prevent this problem? Could you have intervened to deal with it earlier? Did you inadvertently take an action that made it worse? Name your part.

> *I want to acknowledge that I have a part in this. We've had packed agendas for our meetings and have usually skipped any discussion of our people issues. I should have noticed that and suggested we schedule a special meeting. As a result, problems have gotten worse. I apologize for that.*

Apologies can be small, like the one above. However, occasionally, you may see that you've played a big role, and you need to go for a big apology. Watch for situations where this is needed and be courageous if it is. A big apology can change everything. Here's one of the most powerful ones I've seen:

> *Eric sat in my office for the first time. He looked uncomfortable, glancing at the door as if looking for a way out. He assured me that his problem with Mary, the head of the legal department in the institutional bank where they both worked, was unfixable. He looked at me sadly and said, "She hates me. She won't speak to me."*
>
> *When I asked him to explain what happened, he told me a convoluted story I could barely follow. The gist of it was that he'd been frustrated about a lack of action on an important deal. The deal had moved too slowly. Desperate (but against the bank's policy), he'd sought external legal counsel, got the answer he needed, and sealed the deal. Mary was furious. She escalated the transgression to the CEO, and she hadn't spoken to Eric since.*
>
> *Eric assured me that he had to take the action he'd taken. There was no other option. And surely the fact that the CEO had said nothing to him meant that he didn't disapprove?*
>
> *Confused, I asked him to explain it again. He told the story again and painted himself as a hero who'd brought in a big deal*

for the bank. In contrast, he painted Mary as the bureaucrat and the problem in this situation.

However, something didn't work for me—in his rush of words, in his body language, and in his difficulty keeping eye contact with me. And then there was a sudden "ding" in my head, and I knew what needed to be asked. "Just checking," I said. "Did you do the wrong thing here?"

Slowly, he responded, "Yes. I guess so, but I had to."

I asked, "Could you make an appointment with her and sit with her and say what you just said to me? 'I did the wrong thing. I'm sorry.' Then don't say anything else. Just wait to hear how she responds."

Eric protested that she would rip him to shreds. She might yell. She might tell him to get out of her office. But eventually, he decided it was worth a try. Things couldn't get much worse than they already were.

When he came to his next session in two weeks, he had a huge smile on his face.

It turned out that when he'd said those magic words to Mary, all she said was, "Thank you. I shouldn't have escalated it. I should have talked to you. Let's draw a line in the sand and get it right next time."

And that was the end of it. Suddenly, they were fine again.

In this case, that was all it took. Maybe your conversation will be this straightforward. But if it's a more complex situation, you may need to craft a more complex opening statement. So, let's go back to the sample statement from earlier. With all its parts combined, it might look like this:

I just want to take two minutes (no longer) to tell you what's on my mind, and then I'm here to listen.

First, I'd like to share my intent. My intent for this conversation is to understand why the employee engagement scores for our division are the lowest in the company.

It is not my intent for anyone to point fingers or get raked over the coals. We're a team, and we need to come together and be honest about our obstacles. Let's share ownership and fix this so we can get our people engaged and working together.

Some very strong people have left our organization in the past year. The engagement survey shows that people in this group are frustrated, and some are looking for other jobs. More than half say they wouldn't recommend the company. It seems like there is something going on here that we need to explore.

I want to acknowledge that I have a part in this. We've had packed agendas for our meetings and have usually skipped any discussion of our people issues. I should have noticed that and suggested we schedule a special meeting. As a result, problems have gotten worse. I apologize for that.

Let's get started. How can we explain this change in employee engagement?

B. Ask the other person to respond—and listen to their response

Earlier in this chapter, we talked about how critically important it is to listen well. Listening well will make all the difference in how the rest of the conversation goes. Note that this is not the time to move to a solution. At this point, you still need to uncover the real issues.

Here are some tips to listen well:

- **Stay present.** Your mind may race ahead as you are listening while you think of how you will respond. If it does, stop. Be fully present to the other person and their message.
- **Share it back.** It can help to paraphrase what the other person said, both to slow down your mind and to let

them know you've heard them. *So, I'm hearing that every-one who has left cited "more money" as the reason. Is that correct?*

- **Take notes.** First, taking notes is a way to make sure you truly listen. It's a way to stop from jumping in with a response. Second, you can refer to your notes as you speak throughout your conversation with them. If you sense your notetaking makes them nervous, you can make the notes on a shared board, so they can see that you're writing down their story, their concerns, and their understanding.

- **Check nonverbal communication.** Check your body language and your nonverbal messages. Do they show you care? Do you make eye contact, lean in, and nod when you agree? Is your phone on the table? If so, put it away. If you must have it out, apologize and let them know why.

- **Encourage them to share.** Even when they seem to be finished, encourage them to say more, to share completely. I promise you that the real gold usually comes out in the second or third round, well after they think they've said enough.

- **Show empathy.** If they communicate some emotion about an event, you might say something like, "I didn't know you were going through that. That must have been tough."

- **Stay in learning mode.** They may want to move to a solution while they share their messages. In this case, you might say, "We're trying to understand all the issues that got us here. I want to hear your ideas, but let's hold off on solutions until all the issues are out there. Do you think we have it all on the table, or is there more?"

- **Do a final check that you've understood.** Once they've finished, you may summarize again to ensure you've understood what they've said. Then you can invite them to explore possible solutions, which is our next step. Listen as if it all depends on how well you've heard them. Often it does.

C. Explore possibilities

If you've listened deeply, you now understand the problem well enough to explore possibilities. Together, you need to decide if you should continue the conversation. If there's a clear "yes" from all of you, go with it while the energy and goodwill are high.

This is where Eric and Mary were earlier in the conversation above. They'd drawn a line in the sand and felt much friendlier toward each other, more willing to adapt to get a good outcome. They just needed to have a conversation about how they would handle it if the same issue came up again. They were able to move straight to clarity about that.

In some cases, however, it might be time for a break—perhaps just thirty minutes or maybe a day or two.

Some reasons you might decide to wait:

- You don't have all the facts. More research is needed.
- The issues are complex, and you haven't yet agreed about them. It doesn't look like you'll get there without a separate session for this purpose.

- You're exhausted, emotionally or physically.
- They're exhausted, emotionally or physically.
- You or they have limited time before the next appointment. You don't want to run out of time.
- You're hungry. It seems minor, but it's not. You're probably familiar with the concept of being "hangry." Low blood sugar can affect moods. Bad decisions can be made when people are hungry but decide to plow through anyway.

If you decide to wait, determine how long you need, then set a date and time for the follow-up. Don't leave it too long. This is a priority, even if it means you must move something else. Set it up sooner rather than later.

Tips for how to explore possibilities (whether now or later)

State the issue, the intent, and the desired outcome. Sometimes, the last two are the same, like, "We want to work together seamlessly and effectively." Make sure you and the other person are on the same page. Then:

- Start with their ideas and listen. Encourage them to talk, and don't interrupt them.
- Ask to clarify any of their points when needed.
- Build on their ideas and give them credit.
- Share your ideas and ask them for feedback.

This part is a kind of dance—a dance that incorporates shared understanding, mutual purpose, and goodwill. You listen, you check to make sure you understand, you share, you ask for feedback, and you repeat the steps together until you've generated a solution that you both think will fix the issue or solve the problem.

Congratulations. You're nearly there.

Part 5: Agree on next actions and follow up.

As a coach, I've learned that one of the most important moments in any client session comes at the end. We agree, together, about the actions that will be taken before the next session. It's a critical part of accountability. The same is true here. All the empathy, shared truth, generation of ideas, etc., will not matter if no action is taken.

You need to take the time to explore this together. What will they commit to do? What will you commit to do? What could possibly get in the way of the successful completion of the actions? Do all parties have the skills, resources, connections, etc. to make it all happen? You may be tempted to make assumptions that it will all just happen, but this is a trap.

I recently conducted a workshop to coach talented and experienced international women from several countries who were looking for local employment in the US. Looking for employment in the States can be a challenge when you're self-conscious about your grasp of English. While the women were confident and

> ALL THE EMPATHY, SHARED TRUTH, GENERATION OF IDEAS, ETC., WILL NOT MATTER IF NO ACTION IS TAKEN.

clear in the room, they balked when it was time to send emails to potential contacts. At first, I took this to be resistance and possibly procrastination, but it was neither of those. What they needed was to see a draft email, so they could adapt it to their situation. While the email task seemed small to me, it was daunting for someone who wasn't confident about their English and wasn't sure what was appropriate to say.

When the actions are set and you've eliminated as many obstacles as you can, you can look at completion dates and document it all. Even if only two of you are involved, put it all in writing and include how and when you will follow up. Do not skip this step.

Even with documentation, you may have seen beautiful decisions fall apart because of your lack of follow-up. If you've experienced this in the past, search inside yourself to see if you might have an allergy to follow-up. Find a way to ensure this won't happen in this case. Whether it's getting reminders from a colleague or coach, make sure that all the work you've done and the creative solutions you've arrived at together will become reality.

Finally, let's finish the story of Julia, the operations manager, her 2 ½ -year-old with his arm in a cast, and the decision she had to make about whether to send her son back to the preschool. Here's what happened:

Julia took the time to think about what she really wanted to achieve with the preschool. She clarified her intent before returning to talk to the teachers. She decided that her intent was to "make sure this won't happen to my child, or any child, again." With that as her goal, she knew she was doing the right thing for the right reason. She let go of her anger and set up an appointment to speak with the teachers when her son returned to preschool.

When she told them what had happened, initially, the teachers were defensive, which she expected. They immediately tried to put the blame on—wait for it—the child who'd jumped on her son. They wanted to guess which of the children had done it and share their theory with her.

However, with Julia's clean intent, she said, "That's not the point. I don't actually want to know who did it. The point is that it happened during playtime, and not only did you not prevent it, but you also didn't know it happened. There's obviously a problem in the way the children are supervised. And that's what needs to be fixed.

"I want to make sure this never happens to another child. And I know that's what you want, too." And with that, she established a shared purpose with the teachers.

Now, they could work together toward the same outcome. She offered her skills to support them in finding a solution that would solve the problem and not blow their budget. (She was, after all, an operations manager, remember?)

When Julia came to our next session, she reported that she felt strong and powerful because she'd handled it better than she would have in the past. She said, "Before, I would have simply reacted." As a result of her growth, she lost her fear of hard conversations. Julia shared with the group that, with her new confidence, she'd subsequently tackled every difficult conversation she'd previously avoided—well, at least on the job. There was still that one issue with her mother-in-law, but she'd get there.

RISE WITH INTENTIONAL CONNECTION

"I love those connections that make this big old world feel like a little village."

—Gina Bellman

WHEN I CONDUCT a session about networking with corporate women, I like to ask, "How many of you genuinely enjoy attending networking functions where you balance a glass of champagne in one hand as you shake hands with the others and engage in small talk and try to make a good impression?" Usually, only a couple of hands go up. Why do some people enjoy it and do it well, while the rest of us walk in the door and wish we were anywhere else?

I'm often in the second category. However, despite my discomfort with most networking events, I attend them, and I've learned how to make them work for me. I don't think anyone else knows that I sometimes check the clock and wonder if I've been there long enough.

Did you know that it's possible to stop attending networking events and still maintain a robust network? Please indulge me as I share with you:

- How to change the way you think about networking (that includes giving it a new name)
- Why it's essential to connect with others and how that's different from what you might know as networking
- How to find your preferred ways to connect with others
- The four directions of effective connection and how to make them count
- The essential step in connection that most of us get a D- on

CHANGE THE WAY YOU THINK ABOUT NETWORKING

I think we've got networking completely wrong and that we need to reclaim it, reframe it, and rename it.

Reclaim it.

Networking has long been the domain of the schmoozers— easy talkers, small talkers, and people with quick smiles and a knack for a good line or a funny story. But have you noticed that when you meet these people, it feels like you've eaten cotton candy? You take a bite, and it tastes good, but you realize there's nothing there, no sustenance or benefit to the interaction. On the drive home, you feel like you should have enjoyed it, but did you? Did this interaction enhance your life or work?

I think it's time to reclaim networking as an opportunity to learn, grow, and meet people we want to know. And during that time, it's okay to be awkward, sincere, earnest, and even vulnerable with each other.

Reframe it.

Why do you go to networking events in the first place? Perhaps your manager has asked you to represent your organization. So, you try to put your best foot forward and sell your organization and yourself. And as you try so hard to prove your worth to others, you somehow end up in conversations that aren't genuine. If you listen closely, you'll hear the false note you're striking, and so will others. But you pretend to be tone deaf because that's how it's done.

What if you had a nobler purpose at these events? Rather than giving out as many business cards as possible and repeating your memorized elevator pitch, maybe you could look for people you can help in some way, not so much with the services you offer (although that may be possible), but in any way they need. And here's the kicker—with no expectation that they will give back. You can connect for real and genuinely care about the people you connect with. You could "give to give" rather than "give to get."

If that sounds like something you'd like to do, if it sounds more genuine and authentic and joyful, here's the good news: it will also make you one of the best networkers ever because people will trust you. And people want to do business with someone they trust.

Rename it.

Networking is such a snappy little one-word term, but let's look for a better one. At its essence, networking is really about connection. We long for connection and community. So, our challenge (for the rest of this chapter, at least) is to talk about connection rather than the act previously known as networking. I won't use the word networking again, although you will hear me talk about the importance of networks.

WHY IT'S ESSENTIAL TO CONNECT WITH OTHERS

We all have our close circles of connections—families, friends, work colleagues. We're comfortable with them and feel safe with them. Does it really matter if we go beyond that group? Many people don't seem to think so. They prefer predictable, low-risk social lives. But what are they missing?

There are great reasons to extend the reach of your circle and share your life with a larger group of people.

Connections build your business intelligence.

- Your connections can help you share knowledge and ideas, learn new things, and stay informed about changes in your business and industry.

- If you're well-connected, you know who to go to when you need help.

Connections improve collaboration.

- When you know a variety of people, you can look for opportunities to collaborate with them on issues you care about.
- Connected organizations work better. It's easier to get things done.

Connections create opportunities for collegiality.

- The more people you know, the greater the chance you have to develop satisfying relationships with like-minded colleagues.
- You can help others through your connections, and they can help you in return.

Connections can make you more credible.

- Trust can be challenging to build in the workplace, and it often takes years to establish. Others will trust you more quickly if they've met you and know you.
- Connecting builds your brand and raises your profile with others.
- Connecting can help you be more influential. If you're well-connected, you'll have more opportunities to make things happen.

Connections can help your career.

- Your connections can help you find future career opportunities. When I ask clients how they got their current position, most of the time it's been through connections. Someone either told them about the role or put their name forward for a role.
- Your connections may see qualities in you that you didn't know you had, building your confidence.
- If you know the right people, you can get their support for something you'd like to work on or be part of.

Connections can build customer relationships.

- With a wider variety of connections, you have more sources for new customers or clients.
- Great connections with customers can create strong loyalty. They are more likely to stay with you.

The value of weak connections

If you're new to a city or industry, you may feel discouraged that you don't have strong connections. But take heart. There is research that tells us that weak connections may be just as good—and maybe even better.

This idea was identified by Mark Granovetter, a sociology professor at Stanford University who wrote a paper in 1973 called "The Strength of Weak Ties." He surveyed 282 Boston-based workers and found that most of them got their jobs through someone they knew. That's important, but what's even more fascinating is that most didn't get their jobs through people they knew well. In fact, 84 percent got their jobs through someone they saw only occasionally. He postulated that weak ties may be more helpful to our careers than stronger ones. Why might that be?

> CONNECTIONS THAT GO BEYOND YOUR IMMEDIATE CIRCLE INCREASE YOUR OPPORTUNITIES TO CREATE TRUST AND EXPAND YOUR POSSIBLE CAREER DIRECTIONS.

- First, the people in your immediate circle tend to know the same people you do. When we get beyond our immediate circle, the next group of people is much more likely to know very different people. So, the bigger your extended circle, the bigger your opportunities.

- Second, the people in your extended circle may even be more helpful than those who know you well. Friends may worry about how recommending you could affect your relationship. What if you don't impress their employer? Will this reflect on them or affect your friendship? People who don't know you well may be more willing to refer you because there's less perceived risk.

Connections that go beyond your immediate circle increase your opportunities to create trust and expand your possible career directions. In so many cases, these widened connections will enrich your life.

After several months of running a program for international women job seekers who didn't initially know each other, I was fascinated to find the following:

- The women who got jobs during the program landed very different roles than those they thought they wanted at the beginning because they'd given each other ideas for new ways to use their skills.
- The relationships between the women became very strong and supportive. They wanted to help each other find jobs, and they would contact each other when they saw an opportunity that they thought was a good fit.

This is why it's important for you to connect with others. But what if you're an introvert? And what if life doesn't leave you much time to make connections? Perhaps we should explore how to fit connection with your personal style and your life circumstances to achieve the outcomes you need. I call that intentional connection.

Find your preferred way to connect

What if you could create a plan that would help you have the exact networks you want and need—connections that are good for your career, connections that enrich your life, and connections that are fun? You can.

But first, stop and think about what *style* of connection is best for you, at least at this point in your life and career. Your unique approach to connection should take into account your personality and preferences and your life circumstances.

When you adapt your connection style, you'll make connecting more enjoyable and creative because it's tailored to you, not to an outdated notion of what networking should be.

Take a few minutes to consider these two factors:

- **Personality and preferences:** Do you like to connect with others via organized groups versus one-on-one? One influential factor may be where you are on the scale of introversion and extroversion. Are you a clear introvert or a clear extrovert? Or are you somewhere in between, what psychologist Hans Eysenck dubbed an ambivert?
- **Life circumstances:** Do you have very limited time for connection outside work hours? Or are you at a stage in life where you can really go for it?

Based on your answers, you can think about what you want your connection style to be. Below are some possibilities.

Introversion, extroversion, and everything in between

Many people think that only extroverts can be good connectors. They move around the room comfortably and engage with many people, making connection look effortless and fun. You can also be a good connector, whether you're a genuine introvert, an out-there extrovert, or an ambivert.

Common sense may assume that a career in sales would require extroversion. But common sense would be wrong. Adam Grant's research shows that ambiverts are better salespeople than either introverts or extroverts. This may be, he says, because they can switch more easily between talking and listening. They're able to hear their customers' issues and needs and showcase the benefits of their product or service.

Still, there are actions you can take to give you an advantage if you are one or the other.

If you lean toward introversion:

- Prepare for connection in advance. Find out who will be there and learn a little bit about them. LinkedIn comes in handy here. Have some opening comments ready. Stay informed about community and global trends. You don't need to know everything, just a few topics that might interest others. Steer clear of polarizing topics; they are communication minefields.

- Engage in one-on-one meetings or small groups rather than large groups. It may seem less efficient to meet people one-on-one, but it will give you quality time together, and you'll have the opportunity to be direct and deep in your questions. A thirty-minute coffee meeting will provide more opportunity to drill deep than the five minutes you get at an event.

- Ask questions. One advantage of being an introvert is that you don't need to talk all the time. Other people appreciate that. Introverts tend to be better listeners. Take advantage of that. Be genuinely curious and draw people out.

- Use written communication or social media to connect with others. Consider writing a blog, where you can plan and think about what you want to say. You may be inclined to communicate through LinkedIn,

Instagram, specific Facebook interest groups, texting, or email.

Danger zones for introverts:

There are some downsides to being an introvert. Others will sometimes dominate the conversation or talk over you. You may need to have a courageous conversation (see Strategy 4) with those people. If they continue to ignore you, you can tactfully say, "I wasn't finished making my point." Female introverts, in particular, can be seen as demure, lacking confidence, and easy to push past. It's crucial to develop the skill of speaking up.

Let me tell you about Abby, an introverted client who learned that she could become a star connector.

Abby sat in my office in her jeans and a t-shirt. She looked more like a shy grad student than the wife of a senior executive. This was a new kind of coaching relationship for me. Abby had come to me because her husband, Jason, was already my client, and he suggested that she might benefit from coaching. Jason had been recently promoted to the executive team of the high-profile tech company where he'd worked for the past ten years. That promotion felt great to him, but it also had implications for Abby, who was expected to join him at exclusive events that the executive team would attend together with their partners.

Abby's eyes widened as she poured out her fears. "I'm just a technical writer. I spend all day working alone. And I like it that way. Some of these people are serious power couples. They're public figures in business and politics, and I don't do politics except for going to protests occasionally. These are people you see in magazines and on television, not people I talk to.

"And I'll meet them for the first time at the Kentucky Derby. I don't have anything to wear. Look at me. Do I look like I belong in a private box at the Kentucky Derby? I don't know anything about horse racing. I don't even understand why it's a thing. Jason says it's okay if I don't go. He'll make excuses for me, but I know how disappointed he'll be. And this won't go away. There will be more events."

I suggested that Abby might actually be a refreshing change to some of these power couples. Since Jason really needed her there, I thought there were a few actions she could take to make this work.

"Prepare in advance," I told her. "Learn about the horses in the race—and perhaps the owners and jockeys—the history of the event, and what happened last year. Use your curiosity to explore what makes other people love horse racing.

"Research the people who will be in the group. You know a lot about the other executives from Jason, but not as much about their partners. Try to be prepared with a question or two for each of them that shows your interest and curiosity.

"Oh, and find a great hat," I said.

Abby was diligent in her research, and it paid off. She had plenty to talk about and had good questions to ask other people. At our next session, she told me how well it had gone. She got people to talk about themselves, and they seemed to enjoy her questions. A couple of the corporate spouses had invited her for coffee, and one couple had sent them a dinner invitation. She said that Jason was so happy and relieved that she'd faced her fears.

If you lean toward extroversion:

- Enjoy spontaneous connections with many different types of people.
- Participate in large group networks, such as professional associations, where you get to meet a lot of

people at once. Conferences and events will be great for you—even better if you're on the stage.

- Make notes about people and keep them in your contact system. You'll meet so many people that you'll need to make sure you remember important details about them.

Danger zones for extroverts:

Of course, there are also downsides for extroverts, and you should be cautioned against these:

- Unfocused connection. Your work connection needs to be intentional. Although you'd like to talk to everyone, you risk skimming the surface if you do.
- Talking rather than listening. Learn to ask good questions and genuinely listen to the responses.
- Lack of follow-up. You tend to meet so many people and may sometimes offer to reconnect, but then fail to follow through.

Bill Clinton's Rolodex is famous. From the time he was twenty-two, he tracked everyone he met. He wrote down information about them and saved it on his Rolodex. Before an event, he'd search his Rolodex for those who would be there to remind himself who they were and what he knew about them. People were surprised and flattered to be remembered in such specific ways.

You probably don't have a Rolodex, but everyone has some kind of online contact system, even if it's just Google Contacts.

No matter how simple your online contact system is, it's a place to write down details about the people you meet. The challenge, of course, is to do it immediately while it's all fresh in your mind. As an extrovert, you're likely to have many contacts but only limited space in your long-term memory.

If you're an ambivert, which may be around half of the population:

- Pick and choose your approach to connection based on your circumstances and your interests.
- Choose small groups sometimes and large groups other times. You'll be able to go and enjoy connecting either way.
- Talk a lot if you wish, but always listen a lot. Pay attention to the preferences of the other people and adapt to them. Some clients have said that how much they talk depends on their level of knowledge. If the conversation is about their area of expertise, they're comfortable talking. Otherwise, they prefer to listen and ask questions.
- Have an onstage presence at times and a backstage presence as an organizer or convener at others. You can shine in both roles.

Danger zones for ambiverts:

Just like with introverts and extroverts, you'll have some things to watch out for, too.

- Set some boundaries. You may find yourself involved in events because others think it's a good fit for you. People might misread your level of extroversion and enthusiasm because they've seen you in your element and encourage you to be part of a project, initiative, or club that doesn't feel right to you. Listen to yourself. Don't overrule your better judgment.
- Find your right balance. You may love being around people, then suddenly realize your social calendar is overloaded, and you're craving alone time.

If you're an ambivert, you may have the right style to be an effective convener. I'm an ambivert, and I love to be in the middle of things. One way to do that is to bring people together. I don't want others to look to me for the answer, so I'm the person who brings them together to share their stories and find their answers. Here's the first time I discovered this wonderful way to connect:

Early in my career as a coach, I participated in a transpersonal coaching certification course with the late Sir John Whitmore, author of the international bestseller Coaching for Performance. *At the end of the program, John took us through an exercise to show how we could go beyond one-on-one coaching and coach a group of people. He demonstrated this method by choosing a topic for our group: "Be the change you want to see in the world."*

After taking us through a meditation exercise, he asked our group some questions to clarify the impact we wanted to make. We each thought deeply about that impact in silence, writing down our responses. At the end of the session, we shared our results and made commitments to take action. I was stunned by the creative and powerful change initiatives (from local to global acts) that people in the group had generated.

Unlike them, I hadn't come up with an initiative that seemed remotely achievable. I felt terrible. I'd failed the final assignment of the program.

And then I thought, "These people inspire me. I might not have amazing ideas for change, but I'm good at creating a safe space for others. I can do that." I determined then and there to stay with these people as they pursued their commitments.

Somehow, I knew that if I worked with this group, I'd find my path to make a difference while helping the group stay accountable.

If we came together once a month, I thought, we could encourage each other to bring each other's powerful dreams to life. The next day, I sent an email to everyone inviting them to lunch at my office, so we could continue our progress together. About half of the group attended the follow-up lunch. For the next year, we continued our monthly lunches and supported each other. It was inspiring to see everyone (me included) clarify goals for social change, move forward, overcome obstacles, and achieve commitments. And though I didn't know it at the time, it would be the source of long-term friendships and incredible opportunities for collaboration.

If you're an ambivert, you might want to consider convening as a connection strategy. It can be a powerful way to make a difference.

How life circumstances affect your ability to connect

During some stages in life, you'll have less available time for connection with others because of the load you're carrying with home and family. You may envy those who can attend a business breakfast without reworking complex family logistics or those who slide seamlessly from the workday into an after-work drink without having to navigate school pickups and homework supervision. If you're lucky, you have a partner who will share the home and family responsibilities with you. Even with the best of partners, it's still a juggling act.

You need to get very clear about how to spend your available connection time. You don't have time to aimlessly meander. When connection time is tight, these ideas may be helpful:

- **Use work time to connect:** Connection can and should be part of anyone's role, and it's absolutely a good use of your time at work. You may want to carve out a small part of your workday or work week for this purpose. Lunchtimes and coffees are commonly used. One great connector I know sets aside Friday afternoon for short calls to clients and colleagues to share a piece of news, thank them for something they've done, ask if they need anything, or just wish them a happy weekend.

- **Be intentional about virtual connection:** This is critically important if you're in a remote work situation. You can set up short "get to know you" Zoom calls with colleagues you don't frequently see.

- **Use social media:** Set aside daily time on LinkedIn to connect with former colleagues you may have lost contact with.

- **Focus on the few:** This may be the time to go deep with the truly important connections (think about the 80/20 rule) rather than connecting with everyone.

So, what's your preferred connection style? Try writing it out in a statement. Make it fit you and your life. What are some good ways for you to connect? How much time are you able to spend? Some example statements include:

YOU NEED TO GET VERY CLEAR ABOUT HOW TO SPEND YOUR AVAILABLE CONNECTION TIME. YOU DON'T HAVE TIME TO AIMLESSLY MEANDER.

"I'm an introvert with limited time for connection. I'll spend thirty minutes per day connecting with others in ways that feel like good fits (coffees, emails, one-on-one meetings, and LinkedIn)."

"I'm an extrovert with time to connect. The more in-person connection, the better. I can connect outside of work time. I'd like to get involved with at least one large industry or professional association. I'll make sure I connect with someone every day and focus on past colleagues, current stakeholders, and people I need to know. I'll make sure I track my connections and follow up with new and old connections."

"I'm an ambivert with limited available time. To use that time well, I'll explore professional groups, both within and outside of my workplace, mostly those that meet and connect during the workday (although I could schedule an evening once a month if I plan in advance)."

If you wrote down your statement, congratulations on the first step toward your connection plan!

Now, let's look at the four directions of connection, and I'll share some practical ideas for each of them.

THE FOUR DIRECTIONS OF EFFECTIVE CONNECTION

As we talked about at the beginning of this chapter, many of us found traditional networking to be uncomfortable, so we tried not to think about it. We slipped in late to organized networking events, only talked to the people we knew, and left early if we could.

If you want to be a great connector, your approach needs to change. You'll need to imagine a new, better version of yourself as a connector because you know how powerful connections are. You know how enjoyable it can be to have great relationships with others. You know how good it will be for business outcomes to have the right contacts, and you know that your connections will impact your future.

So, how can you do that? You may find it helpful to listen to the advice of the late Stephen Covey to "begin with the end in mind." What do you want to achieve at work, either in the short term or the long term? Make a statement about what you want to achieve in your career, big or small. Then think through how connection can help you get there.

"I want to manage a large team of people focused on improving our digital platforms."

How can connection with others help me get there?

- **Better connections in my area** can enable me to get support and alignment from my team members and close colleagues.
- **Better connections across the business** can help me test the impact of my ideas on others and potentially win them over.

- **Better connections with more senior people** in my business can help me get the go-ahead to proceed and the resources to be successful.
- **Better connections externally** can help me increase my knowledge, credibility, and learn about others' success.

These examples lead us to the four directions of connection:

1. **Connection within**—your business unit
2. **Connection across**—your stakeholders and other parts of the business
3. **Connection up**—more senior people
4. **Connection out**—outside of your business

Let's discuss each of these more.

1. Connection within

The first place to increase your connection might be within your business unit with your direct reports and peers. Some reasons you might need to connect within:

a. **You're new** to your workplace. If you're the newbie, the best start you can make is to understand every role and the people in those roles by taking time to get to know and learn about your colleagues.
b. **You're not new,** but you still don't know all your colleagues as well as you could. Maybe you work remotely or spend a lot of time on the road. Connection with your peers can make the job much more enjoyable and

can even help you support each other seamlessly, so you can pick up and pitch in as needed.

c. **You've been there a while** and think you might be considered for your manager's role one day. If that's a possibility, current peer connections become ultra-important. You'll want your peers to be supportive if they're asked about you (and there's a very good chance they will be). And you'll want them to support you in the role after you get it.

Here's an example of a client who needed to focus on connection within:

Kirk was a top dealmaker for an institutional bank. He had an unsmiling, unblinking gaze that felt like he was looking through me instead of at me. As we discussed the issues that led to his coaching, he explained:

"Look, I'd like to be a nice guy with my coworkers. Deep down, I am a nice guy. But frankly, I don't have the time or the patience. I have to focus on our customers, on finding and designing great deals, and saving deals that are at risk. That's my real job.

"I understand that some people are upset by my directness and sense of urgency; they think I'm too demanding. Apparently, someone's complained about me—again. I've heard this before, so I might as well give coaching a try."

As we dug deeper, I learned that Kirk had alienated many of the people he needed to work with. His manager frequently had to step in to solve disagreements and soothe injured feelings, and she'd had enough. Despite the amount of business he brought in, she was prepared to slash his bonus if he didn't improve his internal relationships.

As we worked together, Kirk learned to connect with the people within his immediate workplace. He started to understand how his colleagues' support contributed to his out-comes. He began to get to know them personally and showed that he valued their contributions—and they responded. To his amazement, work became more enjoyable as he connected in this new way. Every time I saw him, Kirk smiled a little more.

The unexpected outcome was that he was able to bring this way of connecting to his client relationships, as well. He showed me a spreadsheet of his results. Once he started to use this kinder, warmed-up approach with customers, Kirk's success in deals increased quantifiably and substantially.

Your need for connection with your colleagues might not be as urgent as Kirk's, but if you feel you could benefit from better, stronger relationships with colleagues, start here. Below are some practical ways to connect within your business unit:

- Invite others for coffee, lunch, or drinks.
- Schedule one-on-one meetings where you learn about their work and challenges, and then determine how you can offer support. Take time to explore their personal goals and interests.
- Initiate catchups that are get-to-know-you sessions with people you don't see on a day-to-day basis. These can include virtual or in-person sessions.
- Plan team social functions or events, both during and outside of work hours.
- Suggest and offer to collaboratively set up a team-building session. This could be part of a team conference or just a special meeting.
- Arrange some training for the whole team. Choose a practical topic everyone would enjoy and benefit from.

Here's how another client, Teresa, applied some of these tactics:

Teresa's frustration was obvious, even over our Zoom connection. She'd fallen out of love with her job as a senior fundraiser for a global charity. Her passion for the cause was still there, but her manager had created an environment with little interaction between team members who worked remotely in different cities. Teresa knew her work was important to the organization and those it served, and she was achieving her targets, but she felt isolated. Her company had limited travel due to budget-tightening, and she was doing all her work online. She felt she wasn't growing. She had so many ideas about ways they could turn the fundraising dial, but it felt like no one was listening.

Teresa came to me to learn more about leadership and to consider whether a leadership role should be her next step. But she didn't even know if it was possible in her current environment.

Listening to Teresa, I learned how much she loved collaboration. Her happiest achievements at work had all been collaborative, either with coworkers or with clients. But her current role didn't include much of that. I also noticed that she seemed to have strong creative problem-solving skills and a keen interest in strategy. These came together to create qualities of a strong leader. Now, she just needed to get some practice. So, we came up with this plan:

- *She asked her manager if she could design and facilitate a team strategy session.*
- *She went to several colleagues with ideas for collaboration.*
- *She asked for the opportunity to work as a player/coach with team members who could benefit from her experience in other locations.*

When her manager moved on, Teresa got the role as head of the team. Because of her informal leadership and the connections she'd made with team members, she had the support of colleagues who previously might have resisted her promotion.

2. Connection across

There are two ways you might want to connect across in your business:

1. Connect with your stakeholders—people you currently need to collaborate with to get the job done
2. Connect with people in other parts of the business—different business units, locations, or divisions that you may want or need to learn about

Each has a slightly different approach.

Connect with your stakeholders

What is a stakeholder? Within an organization, a stakeholder is anyone who contributes input to the work that you or your team do or anyone who relies on you or your team to contribute to the work they do.

Good stakeholder relationships lead to good business outcomes, and getting stuff done is smoother for everyone. Strong stakeholder relationships can sometimes also create powerful advocates when you need them. It's important to take the time to:

*   Know who your stakeholders are as people, not just functions

- Understand their needs and make sure they understand your needs
- Check in with them periodically to make sure the work is flowing smoothly and all needs are being met

There can be challenges and inefficiencies if you treat your stakeholders as functions that are just there to serve you, as in this example:

A team of insurance claims people spent a lot of time playing the blame game. They blamed their stakeholders for slow response times, which resulted in an inability to meet their deadlines. At a workshop, I asked them each to list their top five stakeholders in other parts of the business.

When they shared their lists, they often listed the functions of *these stakeholders rather than their names.* Why? *I wondered. It turned out that sometimes they didn't actually know the names of their key stakeholders, had never met them, or had never had contact with them beyond department-to-department transactions.*

Clearly, these stakeholder relationships needed some TLC. To warm up these relationships, I asked them to meet with one of their key stakeholders before our next group session. In that meeting, they were to find out more about the other person's role, explore their performance goals, and learn something about them personally.

Afterward, a young claims manager told me, "I'd never met Susan before. When I asked her about her role, I was surprised to learn what else she has to do besides deal with our team's insurance claims. She's working with claims coming in from several other teams and is constantly juggling to meet everyone's needs. Part of her job is to find efficiencies, and as we talked, we realized that we were both frustrated with our clunky systems and processes. They haven't been updated in years. We set another meeting to develop ideas to fix that."

Here are some suggestions for building relationships with stakeholders:

- Identify them, especially the most important stakeholders who can either help or hinder you from getting the job done. (Note: they might be individuals or even whole teams.)
- Meet with them to understand:

  - Their roles in full (not just as their role relates to you).
  - Their criteria for success.
  - What do they need from you to be successful? After you understand that, you can share what you need from them to be successful.

- Set regular check-ins to assess your work together.
- If there's a team of people who are stakeholders (marketing and sales would be an example), consider having a facilitated workshop designed to help your teams understand each other better and generate ideas about how you could collaborate more effectively.
- Do a fun activity together.
- Acknowledge and reward them when they go above and beyond. You could send a thank-you note, post a shout-out, or send flowers. Or if the impact is significant, you could nominate them for a company award.

Connect with people in other parts of the business

Sarah, a coaching client, realized late in her career that she was missing some crucial business background and wouldn't achieve her goals without getting that experience. Here's her story.

Sarah was in her fifties and led a large operational division in a global bank. She was well-respected as a high achiever, happy in her role, and thinking ahead to a future career as a non-executive board director. We started to work together on a plan to help her achieve that future, and she was suddenly struck with a big reality check. When a board recruiter looked at her resume, they told her she wasn't ready for a board role.

The recruiter could see that Sarah had taken on big jobs and had succeeded in her career, but he said that she lacked breadth. Sarah had never had her own P&L division, and she'd never had an international role, both of which were gate-openers for a board position in a global organization.

Sarah was initially daunted, but she was also committed. She needed to focus on connections across the business to better understand global operations and to position herself for a P&L role.

Given that Sarah wanted to make this transition in five to seven years, she needed to move fast. She let HR know that her next move in the company needed to be a P&L or global role, and she asked for their support. She started to build connections with senior people in parts of the business that operated globally. She talked to all the leaders she knew who had P&L responsibilities and engaged them to help her find her path. Finally, she began to update her financial leadership skills.

With her connections, she managed to land a P&L role in a small but highly visible division in another country. She used her operations skills to streamline that business, grew it significantly, and increased profitability during her four years in the role.

A few years later, Sarah landed her first paid board role, and she retired from her executive career. Many years later, she continues to add to her impressive portfolio of companies.

While this wake-up call came to Sarah in her fifties, you can learn from it now. If you want to eventually move up, it's important to understand the entire business and how the various pieces work together.

Many women are content to stay in the same area for their whole careers. They see only one path to growth. And they miss rich opportunities. It's not easy to convince others that you're ready for a significant change, but if you're going to grow, you need to seek out and embrace change when you see an opportunity.

That's why, in some companies, new graduate programs are structured to move new hires around to give them a whole-systems approach to the workplace. In addition, many companies have high-potential programs designed to give leaders of the future solid cross-business exposure. It gets harder as you reach senior levels because you're probably more specialized, which makes it challenging to take on a completely different sort of role. However, even at senior levels, breadth is important. When you're on the executive team, it helps to have a deep understanding of every part of the business, so you can contribute in a meaningful way.

If your company doesn't have a structured program to do this, don't wait. Do it for yourself. Seek out people from other areas and learn from them. What is their organization's vision? What are its key objectives? How is it structured? What is the culture? How does one area contribute to the others? How do they all come together to achieve goals? Seek advice from anyone who can help you understand, not just the top leaders. You can learn a lot about other parts of the business from those who work at lower levels.

Here are some ways to learn about and connect with other business units or divisions:

- *Informational interview:* You can set up a thirty-minute meeting with someone who works in a part of the business you don't know well. Ask them to give you a quick overview of their business, so you can understand their key objectives, customers, and culture.
- *Company-wide town halls:* When you go to these, try to meet people you don't already know.
- *Corporate volunteer projects and fundraisers:* These are often open to the whole business, so get involved.
- *Company networking events:* Most large companies have specific opportunities that bring people together, like International Women's Day or holiday events.
- *Showcase presentations:* Invite people from other divisions to showcase the work they do with your team.

3. Connection up

If your goal is to progress upward in your organization, you must be seen. This includes being visible to more senior people. Some ways to achieve this include:

- **Ask a senior person who's done it before to help you solve a problem.** When you feel stuck on a complex work problem, it can be an opportunity. Look around. Who's been in your shoes in the past? Who might be able to help you? Here are some tips to make it a successful ask:

o   Consider who's done this before. Could it be someone who was in your role five or ten years ago?
o   Is there a more senior manager who's said, "If you ever need anything, let me know"? Now is the time to take them up on that offer.
o   Don't ask for more of their time than you need. If you can do it in fifteen minutes, ask for that much time.
o   Follow up with a thank you, regardless of whether they were able to help. And if you take their advice and get a good result, make sure you share that with them.

- **Be where more senior people will be present.**
There are many ways you can increase your visibility with more senior people:

  −   Speak at business events. If you're someone who can pull off a pretty good presentation, you have a real advantage. When a corporate presentation is needed, most people look hard at their cuticles. You can be the one to speak up and take it on.
  −   Join an Employee Resource Group (ERG) if your company has one. As mentioned previously, there may be groups for women, for people of color, for

ethnicity, for LGBTQ, or for young employees. These groups often run forums across the business and usually have an executive sponsor.

— Write for industry publications. If you're a good writer, this is a great way to increase your visibility. Submit to the most reputable publications—the ones your senior leaders are likely to read.

— Connect with them on LinkedIn. Even if you work in the same company, you're likely to learn something new about them from their LinkedIn profile, and you can respond to their posts. If you respond with enthusiasm and intelligence, they may look at your profile.

- **Ask your manager for opportunities.**
  Many managers recognize the importance of giving visibility to their team members.
  Could you:

  — Present your work at a more senior team meeting?
  — Cover for your manager while they are on vacation?
  — Attend a meeting with them?

- **Ask someone to mentor you.**
  Mentorship is a widely accepted development practice in most organizations. I'll have a lot more to say about mentoring in Strategy 6, but you may be able to get your manager or HR to help you find a mentor, or you can just ask someone directly.

4. Connection out

This is a huge opportunity, and it includes any kind of formal connection outside your organization, such as professional associations, volunteer/charitable groups, conferences, alumni associations, external social media, and more.

You may wonder why you should bother connecting outside your organization. After all, it can be time-consuming. A surprising number of women think their external contacts are primarily for getting a job elsewhere. They're worried that they'll be viewed as less committed to their job if they spend time engaged in external organizations and activities. The opposite is true.

Strong external connections can help you establish credibility in your business. If you know the right people to talk to in industry associations, community organizations, and other companies related to your business, you'll bring valuable information to the table. Plus, if people in your organization see that you're valued externally, they're more likely to take you seriously inside the business.

Because the topic of external connection is large, complex, and rich in variety, it's easy to get overcommitted or overwhelmed with options. You'll want to think about how much time you have, what will benefit you most, and then set up a plan. I encourage you to keep your external connection plan SAFE:

- **Simple:** Don't try to do more than you can. Consider your other commitments.

- **Aligned:** Ask, "How is this of benefit, and how does it align with my interests and values?"
- **Fun:** If you enjoy the process, it will help you overcome the bumps you may encounter.
- **Enriching:** Your life should be better and richer because of the time you spend here. If you don't feel enriched by your external connection, look for other opportunities until you find a better fit for you.

So, what should your plan look like? You may choose to join/attend/do one or more of these:

- **A professional association or alumni association:** Most external organizations have opportunities for you to attend one gathering per month, but more time will be needed if you're involved in leadership (more about why this is a good idea later). Many cities also have professional women's associations, which can connect you with other women in similar fields.
- **A volunteer or charitable group:** This is a great way to represent your employer and meet like-minded people.
- **A conference:** Your business's budget may allow you to attend a relevant conference each year. Or if it's something that will really help you grow, you could even pay for it out of your pocket.
- **Social media:** We're talking business-related social media here, not home gardening solutions. Often, these will be on LinkedIn, but you may find relevant sites on other social media channels. Probably ten to fifteen minutes a day will be enough.

Flex your plan around your preferred connection style, which you learned earlier in this chapter. Make your plan smaller if you have significant parental responsibilities or if you're taking evening classes (which is also a great way to connect with others). Be choosy. Select organizations and events that you care about and that you will find enjoyable. These will keep you engaged for the long term.

Let's look a little closer at these options.

Professional associations/alumni associations

Professional and alumni associations are a great way to learn new things and meet new people. However, if you only attend monthly meetings, it only gets you so far. I encourage you to take the extra step of becoming part of the group's leadership. Why? It's great for your resume and helps you develop additional leadership skills beyond those required in the workplace. It also helps you make broader and deeper connections.

I first learned this lesson from Alex, whom I met in a workshop I conducted for young attorneys. When I told a partner in his firm that my workshop included a session on networking (the word I used in the past to describe connection), he said, "Networking? You've got to meet Alex. He's one of the best networkers in the firm."

I dutifully called to set up an appointment with Alex and expected to meet a seasoned, smooth, successful partner. To my surprise, Alex was in his twenties and—as I found out—just a few years out of law school. We met in his tiny office (rather than in one of the firm's flashy meeting rooms), and he greeted me with a friendly, open smile. He asked questions about the program I was offering, and I asked him how he got his reputation as an expert networker. Here's what he told me:

"When I joined the firm straight out of law school, a partner suggested that I should choose one professional association to join. When you're a junior lawyer, long hours are expected, so she advised me to focus on only one group that I cared about and enjoyed. She also pushed for me to take on a leadership role within that organization.

"I'd enjoyed law school and thought I'd like to be part of the alumni association. So, I joined and asked if they needed additional people on the leadership team. It turned out there were several open roles. After reviewing them all, I decided to take on the role of monthly events planner. I had to set the dates, secure the venues, find speakers for each event, and send out invitations.

"To my complete surprise, I was given a huge confidential file with the names and contact information for every success-ful, visible person who'd graduated from my law school (CEOs, managing partners of law firms, political leaders, heads of non-profits, board members, etc.). I contacted some of them to see if they'd be interested in speaking at a monthly alumni evening, and every single person accepted. Not only that, but they also all agreed to meet with me first, so I could brief them on who would attend and how we'd like them to focus their presenta-tion. Here I was, a brand-new lawyer, suddenly connected with successful, even famous people."

Amazed, I asked Alex whether he'd brought any business to the firm from these new contacts. He told me that he felt it wasn't appropriate for him to pitch business to them because he was there only in an Alumni Association capacity. But he'd stayed in touch with all of them afterward, sent them articles he thought they'd enjoy, and checked in when their name was in the news.

Only a few years later, Alex became the youngest partner his firm had ever promoted.

Learn from Alex and seek a leadership role in whatever organization you join.

Charities/community associations

If you want to increase your connection beyond professional organizations, consider volunteer work or community involvement.

Many organizations enable you to do some volunteer work during your normal work schedule. It's a great opportunity to make a difference and to meet people in the community. My daughter, a writer and editor, runs writing workshops in nursing homes as part of a community initiative, and her organization pays her to do that for a certain number of hours. She finds it deeply fulfilling, gets practice running workshops, and has met community leaders as part of her training and work. It's a win-win.

Conferences

Perhaps your workplace will sponsor you to attend a conference from time to time. If they won't, and you're able to do so, maybe it's worth the investment for you to pay for the conference yourself. You may think that conferences are for learning what's going on in your field. And they are for that, but more importantly, conferences provide a great way to connect with people you might not otherwise meet. And it shouldn't surprise you to learn that you'll have a more powerful experience if you're a conference organizer rather than simply an attendee. Furthermore, you'll generate more credibility as a speaker. (And conferences almost always need organizers and speakers.)

Even if you attend as a participant, you can find out who will be there. This information is often available on the conference app. Figure out who you want to meet. Plan to go early and stay late to get the most out of your connections.

Keith Ferrazzi, in his classic book *Never Eat Alone* (which I refer to as Networking on Steroids), has a great chapter on how to get the most out of conferences. I love his list called "Don't be this person." Here are his five categories with a thought or two of my own for each:

1. The Wallflower: Don't stand in the corner; find someone to talk to. Don't sneak off to your hotel room at the end of the day; instead, meet people during the breaks. Find a group that's going out that evening and ask if you can join. Even if you're an introvert who feels overwhelmed by all that togetherness, you can sneak away for the quiet time you need and return when you're refreshed enough to connect again.

2. The Ankle Hugger: Don't hang around with who you came with. That means don't sit with them at the conference or during breaks and meals unless it's pre-planned. Find new people to meet and socialize with.

3. The Celebrity Hound: Don't be the person who wants to hang out with the most famous person at the conference unless you have a great reason. At conferences, most celebrities are invited to draw attendance, not because they can actually help you grow professionally.

Those opportunities are just as likely to come from the person sitting next to you.

4. The Smarmy Eye Darter: You know this person, the one who doesn't really want to talk to you because they're on the lookout for someone more important or more impressive. Don't be that person. Everyone there is worth your full attention. Sure, you may not want to spend the whole conference with them, but give them your attention while you're together, and then move on politely.

5. The Card Dispenser/Amasser: Business cards may be on their way to extinction at this point, and the quality of your conference experience has never been about the number of business cards you collect. It's always been about real relationships—relationships that will be continued. Conferences are great opportunities for building those relationships. Remember that a few genuine connections can be more valuable than dozens of contacts you've forgotten by the end of the day.

Social media (outside your organization)

Unless you're living in a cave, you already know how addictive social media can be. But this is one time you might be able to make that addiction work for you. The challenge is to engage in social media that also professionally enriches you. By all means, if you love Facebook, Instagram, YouTube, or whatever the social media du jour is, enjoy them on your own time. Maybe they can be useful professionally, but don't try to fool yourself if they aren't.

In the business world, LinkedIn is currently the most effective way to network online outside of your workplace. It allows you to stay in touch with former colleagues and managers, and to connect with nearly anyone you meet through conferences, events, or organizations.

LinkedIn has plenty of guidelines to help you create a strong profile, make connections, respond to posts, and post content. In addition, some coaches can help you use LinkedIn, but it's easily accessible for most people's needs.

FOLLOW-THROUGH

This is the one in which most of us get a D-. The exceptional connectors I've learned from always talk about the importance of follow-through. It's the critical success factor for getting it right. Even if you've never been good at follow-through—*especially* if you've never been good at follow-through—this message is for you: none of this will work unless you keep at it daily, weekly, monthly—relentlessly.

Follow-through is up to you. Period. If you want to know that person, you need to let them know that's what you want.

> **NONE OF THIS WILL WORK UNLESS YOU KEEP AT IT DAILY, WEEKLY, MONTHLY—RELENTLESSLY.**

I learned this the hard way. I've attended conferences and events, and I've let magical, full-of-potential opportunities fall through because I didn't follow through. These missed opportunities were often with people I needed to know or relationships that could have developed into business opportunities. At times, it felt like the universe had proffered exactly what I needed, but I didn't take advantage of what was there. Much of the time, I came away with a stack of cards that, years later, ended up in the recycling bin.

I hope you won't let that happen to you. I know you're busy and have immediate, pressing priorities that get in the way. After being away, you return to an overflowing inbox and urgent deadlines, so those take over. That's why I think you'll like these tips about how to turn contacts into real, ongoing connections.

1. **Connect immediately** on LinkedIn when you meet someone you want to know. If you've made a commitment to send an article or set up a Zoom call or meet again in person, make a note of it in your first message to them and track the commitment for yourself (see the next item).

2. **Create a follow-up system that works for you.** You must have a way to track your high-priority connections. Some track their connections in a special physical binder or keep a page on their laptop. You could use an app or a journal. Whatever you choose, this is your personal system to help you stay connected, not just once but for as long as you consider them to be people you want to know. For example, your system might show:

   - When you connected
   - Personal information about the connection
   - When you need to connect again (and don't forget to put this in your calendar)

3. **Make time.** If possible, set aside enough time after the event to follow up. Maybe you need to dedicate a full day after attending a conference or a couple of hours after shorter events.

4. **Keep it real.** When you make contact through email or LinkedIn, be sure to include something personal and genuine. Don't even think about sending a standardized note to everyone. Remind them of what you talked about, what you found interesting about them, and even tell them about an action you took that they suggested. Track it and make a note in your system about when your next contact will be.

Follow these, and you'll improve your connected life.

In our next strategy, we'll look at another form of connection and some of the most powerful connections you'll ever have: your allies and champions.

RISE THROUGH ALLIES AND CHAMPIONS

"What we most want in life is someone who will make us do what we can."

—Ralph Waldo Emerson

EVERYONE NEEDS SOMEONE to support their growth. In an ideal work world, you'd have someone in your life who sees your potential, encourages you, shows you a great career path, guides you through tough situations, advocates for you with others, lets you know when you're off track (and shows you how to get back on), and points you toward opportunities that will help you grow.

I believe that, in exchange for your labor and in addition to fair financial compensation, these are akin to human rights. You deserve this kind of support, but do you get it from your managers? Rarely. A few times in your career, you might strike gold and work for someone who realizes that helping people grow is a significant part of their leadership role. They foster your growth. They help you find your edge. They challenge you and stimulate you.

However, most of the time, managers are focused on achieving the outcomes they've been assigned. As a result, they delegate to you so you can help them get their job done. They're not bad people. They don't want you to flounder. They simply have scarce resources, limited time, and a lack of awareness about how they can get the most from the people who work for them. For many, delegation is their only leadership skill.

So, what should you do? Go find another manager? That's not easy to do, and it's not necessary. Instead, you can learn the skill of self-leadership. The truth is that no one cares about your growth as much as you do. Therefore, you need to own your path.

Years ago, I read a book by a successful woman executive (book title and author name long forgotten) who wanted to share her experience and advice with her daughter. Much of the advice was dated to an almost scary extent. (Extreme example: a colleague once showed up at her hotel door buck naked. Her advice was to act flattered but tell him she had a "no relationships at work" policy.) Despite this, I felt compelled to read on. This had been her reality. This was what she had to endure to be an executive in the 1950s and 1960s.

One piece of her advice jumped out at me, and I saw its truth: as much as possible, treat your job as if you own it. This blew my twenty-something mind. There was no way I could own my job. I worked for the company, had a manager, was subject to numerous rules and policies, and I was paid. I had, I thought, no control. They owned me.

However, once I applied the own-your-job rule, things started to change. I saw what was possible in my workplace and what was

THE TRUTH IS THAT NO ONE CARES ABOUT YOUR GROWTH AS MUCH AS YOU DO. THEREFORE, YOU NEED TO OWN YOUR PATH.

needed to make it better, more efficient, more enjoyable, and more connected. When I stopped caring so much about policies (the way it's always been done) and worried less about what others thought of me, I became increasingly powerful inside and outside.

I'll say it one more time: No one cares about your growth, aspirations, fulfillment, or happiness as much as you do. The sooner you start to own your career, the better.

That doesn't mean you'll have to do it all yourself. It does mean that you'll need to find people who will nurture your development. So, let's focus on how you can find the support you need and long for. The list below takes it from the easiest to the hardest, but often the most rewarding, to find.

1. ROLE MODELS

This person is an example to you. The life you see them leading is one that excites and inspires you. It could be a well-known person who publicly stands for what you want to stand for. In this case, you probably don't know the person, and you may never know them. Or they might be closer to home, like someone in your organization or field who consistently gets it right. Either way, you make the choice to learn from them.

A role model has qualities you'd like to develop in yourself. It could be their values, their business acumen, their presence, their ability to overcome obstacles, or the way they navigate change. As a role model, anyone can be your guide. You don't need their time, and you don't need their permission to learn from them. And you don't need to interact with them at all, although it's possible that you may, at some point, have the opportunity to do so.

There are limitations to what you can gain from a role model. Without any interaction, you won't be able to ask questions or seek their advice on a specific matter. And in most cases, there won't be an opportunity for them to see you or your work.

There are two kinds of role models: those you can observe up close in your organization or other parts of your life, and those you will need to observe from afar, such as famous people, CEOs, etc.

Role models nearby

Let's say your role model is a senior leader in your company, someone you can't access because of the disparity in your level or because they're in a different part of the business. There are still many ways you can learn from them. Here are a few:

- Connect with them on LinkedIn. If they post on LinkedIn, you can follow them or check to see what they've posted lately. If you like what they say, respond with a comment of support. Their LinkedIn profile will also give you a good idea of the path they've taken in their career, what others say about them, and who they follow on LinkedIn.
- Get to know someone who works for them. This is a great way to find out specifically how they work and lead.
- Attend functions where they speak. You'll learn from them through the stories they share and the examples they provide. Some companies will host "Get to know x" events, where a leader is invited to share their background and career path and answer questions.
- Observe the decisions they make and the way they communicate.

Role models at work can sometimes lead to greater connections. You may have an opportunity to meet and get to know the person through a project or an employee action group, and when you do, you can share that they've been your role model. Or, as your career progresses, you may find another way to meet them.

Here's a story about Penny, a coaching client. When we started, Penny was struggling in her job, and she used a role model to help her get through that difficult time with an unexpected outcome.

Penny was new to a leadership role she'd suddenly inherited when her manager abruptly left the organization. The promotion was a significant leap from the narrowly focused role Penny had previously held. Others were excited for her, but Penny was miserable. She oversaw an organization that was in chaos and full of underperformers who hadn't been held accountable for years. Her area was badly in need of a significant cleanup, and Penny felt painfully out of her depth. In addition, her home life was a juggling act. She had two toddlers and a baby and was the primary income earner for her family. She was desperately afraid of losing her job.

Penny didn't have a mentor in the organization and was afraid to ask colleagues for help while she had so many problems and insecurities. There was someone she greatly admired, though. A senior leader, Elizabeth, had also been rapidly promoted and, like Penny, had a young family. Penny took courage from their similarities. She appreciated Elizabeth's integrity and authenticity, her caring nature, and her ability to stand her ground with grace. She saw that Elizabeth lived her values in a challenging environment. Because Elizabeth was in a completely different type of work (Penny worked in finance, and Elizabeth was in customer strategy), Penny didn't approach her to be a mentor. Instead, she decided to observe Elizabeth and to watch and learn.

As I worked with her, Penny looked at her options. She spoke openly and honestly with her manager about her experiences in the job, and eventually, she moved on to a different organization and a new role that was much more in line with her strengths. After she landed the new role, we celebrated after work with a glass of champagne at a local wine bar. As it happened, Elizabeth was also there, waiting to meet someone else. Penny took that opportunity to share with Elizabeth that she'd been her role model and had inspired her through a tough time.

Fast forward several years, and Elizabeth was the CEO of a large business. By this time, Penny had moved up repeatedly and experienced success in a senior leadership role, and she'd never forgotten her admiration for her role model. When a position on Elizabeth's executive team came up, Penny jumped at the chance to apply—and she got the job.

Role models you observe from afar

Famous people, of course, can make great role models. We've all been teenagers, after all. Who didn't find an actor or musician or another famous person we admired and couldn't get enough of through social media, articles, and news?

As you probably already know, most stars have whole teams of people who help create their images, and you can never know what's true about them and what isn't, particularly from social media. Watch out for those who project admirable qualities they don't really have—celebrities with a PR team and the Instagram influencers who have someone else write their copy.

However, there are ways to learn about your far-away role models.

- **Biographies, memoirs, and autobiographies:** One of my role models is Indra Nooyi, chair of PepsiCo. Why? Not because I aspire to do what she's done (her path is well beyond my reach), but because her values and vision have long inspired me. She navigated an unlikely path from an insular life in India to become the CEO and later chair of an iconic global company. She was challenged repeatedly but stayed true to both her personal and professional values while maintaining a stable marriage and having two daughters. She designed and led a strategic vision of Performance with Purpose. She saw the future of PepsiCo as a purpose-driven company. This meant a commitment to deliver financial results in a way that was good for the company and good for the world. There were many ways PepsiCo pursued this. One way was Indra Nooyi's vision to change the balance of its products to nutritious snacks and beverages. Ultimately, these have become their most important products.

When her autobiography, *My Life in Full: Work, Family, and Our Future,* came out, it resonated with truth and authenticity. It was a story of grit, tenacity, and purpose. Chances are that I'll never meet Indra Nooyi, but I've learned so much about leadership from her.

- **Master classes:** When people reach a certain stage in their career, they may share what they know through a master class. This is an incredible way to learn. It's almost as if you were in the room with them. Master classes can be in person or online.

- **TED talks and podcasts:** Your role model may have given a TED talk, which is a great way to learn about their point of view on particular topics. In addition, it's likely that others have interviewed them on podcasts, which is a great way to hear their responses to questions you'd like to ask them.

- **Contact with the author of a book you love:** Many people post Amazon or Goodreads reviews or may even post on the author's Facebook page or website, but few make direct contact with the author. Most authors appreciate direct, positive feedback, particularly if their book has changed your life in a specific way.

I read Raj Sisodia's wonderful book *Firms of Endearment* when it was first published in 2007, and I found myself so inspired by the idea of purpose-driven business that I tracked him down through a friend who'd studied under one of his co-authors. I emailed Raj, saying that his book had inspired me to change the direction of my consulting work. I said that his book had flipped a switch in me from off to on. His response was warm and welcoming, and he invited me to learn more about the Conscious Capitalism movement, which he had co-founded based on the ideas in that book. I became a member of that movement and, within months, attended a conference in Boston. Not long afterward, I co-founded a chapter of Conscious Capitalism in Australia and later another one in Portland, Oregon. I transitioned from being Raj's admirer to being his active supporter and friend, with many wonderful opportunities in the process. Through this work, I had the opportunity to run conferences, lead workshops, work on culture programs in businesses, and coach leaders to find their purpose.

I never even expected a response to that email, but it started one of the most joyful periods of my career. It can be exciting and enlightening to learn from role models. It's such an easy way to learn and grow from great people.

2. ACCOUNTABILITY PARTNERS

An accountability partner is someone who will help hold you accountable to do the work you want to do.

As I write this, I am, at this very moment, tapping into the support of accountability partners. I'm a participant in an online "Get It Written" Day that author C.J. Hayden holds monthly.

Each day has a theme and encouragement from C.J., and participants share with each other what they intend to write (pages, projects, blogs, posts, emails—the list is different for everyone). Then the participants disappear, write for ninety minutes, and reappear to share that they achieved their objective (or didn't), and get a pep talk from C.J. They then rinse and repeat two more times, making it nearly a full day of writing and inspiration.

Here's what Tara Mohr, author of the bestselling book *Playing Big* has to say on the subject of accountability, "When there's a difficult email I have to write or a difficult phone conversation to have, I often check in with a friend who lives across the country, tell her what I need to do, and that I'll call her when it's done. She does the same with me. We move forward on things we'd otherwise avoid endlessly. Over the years, I've learned that when I'm accountable to someone, *wow, do I behave differently*—consistent action happens, resistance is overcome, behaviour patterns change."

Tara also points out many other ways (in-person working groups, online working groups, monthly dinners) in which her colleagues and friends came together to hold each other accountable for achieving stretch goals.

There is also empirical support that accountability partners make your success (much) more likely: an Association for Talent Development (ASTD) study is widely cited as showing:

- You have a 65 percent chance of completing a goal if you commit to someone.
- If you set a specific accountability appointment with someone else, your chance of successfully completing a goal increases to 95 percent.

Your accountability partner will normally be someone who's already in your life (therefore not hard to find) and will be an important ally in your success. Here are a few key factors that will enhance the partnership's success.

- **Choose someone who will commit.** Marshall Goldsmith, award-winning coach and prolific author, shared at a workshop that for many years, he and his accountability partner texted or spoke every single day, sharing whether they had achieved their goal for the day, and then committed to what they would do for the following day.

    You may not want a daily partner (weekly may work for you), but make sure you don't choose a partner who will drop the ball when they don't hear from you.
- **Choose someone who won't let you off the hook.** Sometimes, people who love you have a built-in ambivalence about your goals. They want you to go out for ice cream with them rather than staying to finish the edits. They want you to play. That's wonderful, but

you don't want to be "forgiven" when it's something you really want to achieve. You need an accountability partner who will be tough (in a kind way) with you.

- **Offer the same support to them to help them achieve their goals.** Accountability works best when it benefits both parties.

3. ADVOCATES

This is just what it sounds like—a person who advocates on your behalf. Peers, colleagues, your manager, customers, and even someone who saw you give a presentation can be advocates.

Advocates are, simply put, those people who will speak up for you. Your relationship with advocates is more personal than with role models because advocates have probably seen you in action.

Who could be an advocate?

An advocate can be anyone who knows you, has worked with you, or has been the recipient of your work and speaks positively about you to others. Chances are, you've had several advocates in your career.

Your advocate may be senior to you, or they may be at the same level in the organization as you. A direct report may serve as an advocate. Peers who have worked with you extensively may be advocates. Customers can be powerful advocates.

You have little control over what other people say about you when you're not around, but you can certainly create an environment that makes advocacy more likely. To create that environment, you must deliver consistently, communicate effectively, and genuinely be there to serve.

The right advocate at the right time can make all the difference. Advocacy has played a larger role than any other guiding principle during my career, often in unexpected ways. Here's an example:

> I was once asked to run a career development program for a group of secretaries and executive assistants at a Sydney-based utility. I threw myself into designing a series of workshops that could help them grow in their professional admin careers.
>
> One quiet, young secretary named Cindy was clearly finding the program helpful. An immigrant, she was new to Australia, and her English wasn't perfect, but her thoughtful intelligence shone through as she stayed after the sessions to ask questions.
>
> As much as I enjoyed running the program, I saw it as a stand-alone project and didn't think much more about it. A couple of months later, I got a call (seemingly out of nowhere) from Victor, the head of engineering for the same utility. He said he'd heard about my work and asked if I'd talk to him about designing and running a professional leadership development program for the managers in his engineering group. This was a big deal. I'd never designed a comprehensive leadership program before.
>
> When I arrived for the appointment, I sat nervously in the lobby, wondering how this opportunity had arisen. To my surprise, Cindy came to the lobby to show me in to meet Victor. As it turned out, Cindy worked as Victor's administrative assistant. After the secretaries' program was finished, she shared with Victor what she had learned about customer service, how to speak up at work, and how to grow professionally. He liked Cindy's description of the workshop. He invited me to design

and run a comprehensive program for his full leadership team of more than eighty leaders, a program I ran over the next six months, and the biggest single project I'd ever had.

Cindy, a young admin assistant, had advocated for me in a way I'd never dreamed she would.

Some tactics to encourage advocacy

In the story above, Cindy's advocacy came as a complete surprise to me. But it's possible to cultivate advocacy. Here are some ways to do that. At this point, if you've read the previous strategies, some of these ideas will sound familiar. But they are worth repeating here. And there are a few new ways we haven't covered yet.

1. **Play to your strengths.** Know what you're good at and demonstrate that through your actions. Go the extra mile. Others aren't likely to advocate for you if you stick stubbornly to your job description. (See Strategy 1.)
2. **Take a stand for something important.** People are more likely to advocate for those who have a clear idea or focus they can get behind. (See Strategy 2.)
3. **Showcase what you stand for.** Speak. Write. Bring people together. Make yourself visible. (See Strategy 3.)
4. **Step up, open up, and speak up.** All of these reflect that you are a person of courage. You'll take on the hard task, communicate honestly and authentically, and say what needs to be said. (See Strategy 4.)

5. **Develop lots of genuine connections.** Put simply, the more people you know, the more potential advocates you'll have. (See Strategy 5.)

6. **Be a warm, friendly, caring person.** Wait a minute. Being a nice person shouldn't come into the equation, should it? Maybe not, but it does. Have you ever thought about acknowledging someone publicly who has done good work but has been a complete asshole to you and others? Did you end up advocating for them? I don't think so. It's much easier to advocate for someone when you know they're a good human being.

7. **Advocate for others.** The principle of reciprocity is one of the key pillars of influence, as shown by Robert Cialdini in his classic book *Influence: The Psychology of Persuasion*. Research shows that people want to help you if you've already helped or supported them in the past. If you advocate for someone else, that person is more likely to advocate for you in the future, maybe at a time when you need it the most. Perhaps you spoke up on their behalf once when they had a visible failure on the job. A year later, you need their support for a project. They feel confident and trust in you, and don't hesitate to support you.

8. **Finally, if you need advocacy, ask for it.** Sometimes, you can just come out and ask someone to advocate for you, like when you're about to apply for a job or need their support on a project. In my experience, other people often don't realize the difference their support would make, and therefore don't think to offer it, even though they would be very willing to do so. If you

know of potential supporters who could help, it may be worth asking them directly. Here's an example:

Lena led talent retention at her law firm, but she was fighting an uphill battle to gain traction on a comprehensive survey she wanted to conduct to understand why they were losing so many young associates. Some older partners thought this was a waste of money, and they objected to what they saw as coddling young attorneys. These partners had been expected to buck up when they were young, with long hours and huge demands, and didn't want a survey to tell them the firm needed to make it easier for the new ones coming through.

Lena knew there were a couple of very senior and successful partners who were quiet supporters of young associates. One of them had been through a divorce early in his career because of the relentless demands of the job; another had experienced a complete health breakdown after coming straight back to work after maternity leave. They wanted to do something to make their firm a better place of work for everyone.

Lena went to her quiet supporters and asked if she could quote them in an article for the next firm newsletter. She explained what a difference it would make if others saw their comments about why they needed to make the firm a better place to work, together with Lena's research on industry loss of talent and the underlying human issues behind it. The partners agreed, and when the newsletter was published, many more partners became willing to support the survey.

Which of these tactics could you employ to nurture advocacy at work?

4. MENTORS

A mentor, by definition, is a more experienced person who shares the benefits of their experience with a less experienced person. They are formally entrusted to provide you with guidance and advice. Typically, a good mentor is knowledgeable in your field and has more wisdom and experience than you do. In most cases, you meet with your mentor on a regular basis. Being a mentor is an act of generosity. Most mentors don't expect a tangible return on their investment.

This concept has captured the attention of the business world for many years with mixed results. Most large organizations have experimented with formal mentoring programs. These may be part of "high potential" programs designed to develop employees who have been identified as future leaders or achievers. Sometimes, they've been a key part of the organization's efforts to develop women and marginalized groups.

Formal versus informal mentoring

When I ask my clients about whether formal mentoring programs have helped them in their careers, I get responses that range from an enthusiastic "yes" from a few to a more common response along the lines of "meh."

Companies that structure in-house mentoring programs face a few challenges:

- The chemistry may not work. What looks good at first blush is often not what works in real life. Mentors and mentees need to have enough common ground to sustain them as they work together. Mentoring relationships often work better when both parties share similar careers, life journeys, and values. And, in this type of relationship, it really helps if they like each other.

- Mentees may defer to the power differential. Ideally, the mentee will attend the scheduled meetings with a clear plan and a specific request for the help they need. Sometimes, however (based on the way things are done in hierarchies), they sit back and allow the mentor to take the lead.

- Mentorship requires time. If the mentor doesn't make mentoring a priority—and as senior people, they have many competing priorities—they may struggle to find time for regular sessions.

- Psychological safety is vital. Either or both parties may come to mentoring with a sense that it isn't safe to be vulnerable. If they aren't willing to share their fears and failures and only focus on successes, some of the most powerful learning opportunities will be missed.

- There's a tendency for formal mentoring relationships to peter out over time. To be fair, this can also occur with informal mentoring. Mentors and mentees may transition to new roles and even new employers, making it challenging to maintain the relationship.

For all the above reasons, you may find that your best bet to land a great mentor may be for you to take the lead and identify a person you want to work with. You can approach your potential mentor with a clear idea of why you've chosen this person and why you would value their support. It can help if you know each other and have established some level of connection and trust, but that's not always necessary.

So, how do you find the right person?

What to look for in a mentor

A mentor could be anyone you know whom you think you could learn from. What should you look for? Someone:

- Senior and more experienced than you, not necessarily older; but they have mastery they can pass on to you
- You admire and feel an affinity for
- Who has some (not necessarily all) of what you need or want to learn. Don't expect them to have everything you need. Such a perfect person probably doesn't exist.
- Who has the bandwidth to be a mentor. You both need to make sure you understand and agree to the time commitment.

In an informal mentoring relationship, the mentee typically initiates the relationship. Most senior leaders would hesitate to offer to be a mentor to you because it can feel presumptuous, so you will need to ask. Keep in mind that if they don't know you, they won't automatically know your needs. However, they can still be a great mentor, as in Patricia's case, below.

Patricia, who worked in a global pharmaceutical company, was seen as a high performer in her operations role. She started coaching because she had recently felt bored and underutilized.

However, she told me how inspired she'd felt when she heard a senior executive speak about the importance of strategy and execution.

"There's nothing much in my job that brings me joy anymore. But this guy really cared. It was all over him," she told me. She'd never felt that she had much to do with the organization's strategy, but after his talk, Patricia was on fire. She felt that she had the potential to be a strategic leader.

I suggested that she could invite this executive to mentor her. She could ask him to help her think more strategically, introduce her ideas, and explore the next steps in her career.

Initially, she was shocked at the idea. "He's not in my world at all, and he's a senior executive, based in another country. How could I ask him?" And then she slowly recalled, "But he did give us his email address and really encouraged us to contact him if we had any questions. Maybe I could do it."

She wrote a draft email saying how inspired she'd felt and asked if he would meet with her. However, she didn't send it until she happened to have a conversation with someone in the company who knew him and told her that he loved mentoring younger people.

She sent the email and received a reply from him in an hour, and they set up what was to be their first mentoring session.

How to ask someone to mentor you

Here are some tips for your initial approach to a potential mentor:

- Start with an email, as Patricia did, and ask to set up a brief online meeting. Or you could suggest a coffee if they are nearby.

- When you meet, let them know why you would like them to be your mentor. What specifically do you admire about them?
- Explain what you would like to learn from them. What guidance would you like?
- If they say yes, ask them how often they'd like to meet. Have a cadence in mind in case they ask what you prefer. Monthly or quarterly are good options.

How to use your mentor effectively

It's valuable for both the mentor and mentee to have some training in what can make the relationship successful. However, if training is not available, here are some ideas. Once they've agreed to be your mentor, you'll probably need to take the reins. This can seem counterintuitive, since the mentor is likely to be senior to you. However, it's your job to create the space for this to be a positive relationship. Your role will be to:

- Initiate meetings with a simple agenda
- Prepare for each session carefully and have questions
- Stay in touch between sessions if appropriate
- Try their suggestions and let them know you tried them and how their suggestions worked out
- Express gratitude for the time they spend with you

Finally, you should get to know your mentor as a person. Be curious about their career and their life. This will make it much more likely that the relationship will last.

Should you find a mentor who looks like you?

Most of us prefer to be mentored by someone who's similar to us. If possible, try to find a mentor who has grown in the ways you want to grow or who has dealt with the challenges you're dealing with now. If you're a marketing professional, you may want to target a more senior marketing person. If you're a working mother, you may want to learn how another woman has navigated motherhood and career successfully. If you're a woman of color, you may want to work with someone you can talk with openly about how to deal with the bias you may be experiencing.

However, this can be hard for women, and particularly for women of color. In many industries, white men still dominate the executive suite and boards. Often, those who can help you the most don't look like you. You need to consider them in your pool of potential mentors.

Most importantly, know what you want to learn, and choose a person who can help you in that way.

5. COACHES

Coaches are people you or your company pays to help you grow. They may support you to develop a specific skill, change a behavior, or help you grow as a leader. A professionally qualified coach is trained to help you be the best version of yourself.

Coaches work with you to develop skills or behaviors that will help you to be successful in your career. A good coach will help you clarify what you want and guide you in figuring out how to achieve it. They'll tap into your strengths and address those pesky weaknesses. They'll hang in there with you through hard times and celebrate wins with you. With a good coach, you'll have the support to go further faster.

A coach will help you take actions you might not have taken otherwise. When I first got a personal fitness coach, she took me outside and told me to run up and down the same hill until I couldn't take another step. As I gasped for air and clutched my sides and practically crawled back to her studio gym, she (a true athlete) smiled ruefully at me and said, "I wish I could make myself do that. But I'll only do it if a coach makes me do it."

Aha! I immediately realized that it's like the work I do with clients.

As a coach, I sometimes encourage my clients to take a specific action that is beneficial for them but also challenging. Let's say they realize that they owe someone else an apology for the way they spoke to them in front of others. My client knows it's the right thing to do, but without someone helping them practice and holding them accountable, they'll find ways to rationalize and avoid it. They'll convince themselves that they shouldn't have to initiate that hard conversation. But because they're working with a coach, they agree to do the hard thing.

Then the coach will stay with them and check in either by email or at the next session to see if they've done it. They learn by doing it until they've developed that particular muscle and can do it for themselves.

One of my clients recently got a significant promotion that she'd worked hard for and deserved. But she told me that without her coaching, she'd still be talking to her friends and family about how hard she'd worked without getting any recognition. She'd still be waiting for someone to see her achievements and promotable qualities. However, because she was working with me, she received the nudge to have the necessary conversations, and she had someone to work with as she practiced those conversations. She did every bit of the work, but the coaching helped her take the steps she needed to take.

Coaching (whether life coaching, business coaching, or leadership coaching) can help you in any of these situations:

1. **You find yourself in a situation in which you don't know what to do.** A good coach won't tell you what to do, but they will help you explore issues and options and arrive at your decision. They might suggest that you:

   - Seek needed data, facts, or information
   - Talk to other people who have expertise or experience
   - Check in with what your experience—and your gut—tells you
   - A good coach won't let you skip over things you don't want to think about. They'll make sure you've done your due diligence.

2. **You know what to do, but you don't have the skills to do it.** Your coach may help you develop those skills,

or they may help you figure out where you can get them.

3. **You know what to do, and you have the skills to do it, but you need someone to help you create your plan and hold you accountable.** This is the most common role of the coach, and it's just as valuable as the first two. Your coach helps you come up with the right approach, summon up your courage, and take action, and they stand with you as you do it. Too many of us have sat on a procrastination fence for months— or years—at a time. Life is too short and too precious to let it slip past while you're stuck.

A coach is different from the other champions (role models, accountability partners, advocates, mentors, and sponsors) because normally, a coach is the only one who will be paid to help you. If your organization pays for coaching, they may have a panel of approved coaches they use and give you some options to choose from. Some organizations now have in-house coaches you can tap into. Some only offer coaches for leaders and high-potential employees. A rare few make coaching available for everyone.

> TOO MANY OF US HAVE SAT ON A PROCRASTINATION FENCE FOR MONTHS— OR YEARS—AT A TIME. LIFE IS TOO SHORT AND TOO PRECIOUS TO LET IT SLIP PAST WHILE YOU'RE STUCK.

In the absence of a coach from your organization, you can decide to pay for coaching for yourself. If you do, it's important to check the credentials of the coach and make sure they have training and experience. You may also talk to someone the coach has worked with previously, so you can get a feel for whether they are the right fit for you.

6. SPONSORS

A sponsor actively takes you under their wing. They want you to succeed and are willing to link their success to yours. They see something special in you and try to help you get opportunities, experience, and resources so you can be successful. If you haven't ever thought about sponsorship, you're not alone. Many people have no idea that sponsorship (for some fortunate people) goes on behind the scenes. It's time to raise this opportunity to the forefront of your awareness.

Sponsorship has been one of the most exciting discoveries I've shared with my clients. When the women I work with learn about sponsorship, they often think it's a special perk for other people, not them, but they're wrong. If you're in a mid to senior role in business, there's a good chance that you have a sponsor now but aren't aware of it. And it's even more likely that you've

> NOT ONLY DOES A SPONSOR OFFER ADVICE AND TALK YOU UP, BUT THEY ALSO CAN EFFECTIVELY PULL YOU UP THROUGH THE RANKS OF THE ORGANIZATION. THEY CAN MAKE VALUABLE CONNECTIONS AND CREATE OPPORTUNITIES FOR YOU. WHO WOULDN'T WANT ONE OF THESE?

had a sponsor in the past but haven't realized it. As Sylvia Ann Hewlett, author of *Forget a Mentor, Find a Sponsor,* says: "Everyone who has realized an amazing vision or exerts remarkable influence can and will point to a series of sponsors, powerful individuals who helped pull them up or fund their ventures or clear a path forward. There are no exceptions."

As you learn more about sponsorship, you may be able to identify someone who is sponsoring you. If so, good for you. You'll learn how to see and acknowledge that sponsor so you can use this important relationship with wisdom, generosity, and gratitude. For those of you who don't have a sponsor, you'll learn how to become more sponsorable so you can attract the right person into your world. And, as you will see, you can benefit from having more than one.

What is a sponsor?

A sponsor is more than an advocate and more than a mentor. Not only does a sponsor offer advice and talk you up, but they also can effectively pull you up through the ranks of the organization. They can make valuable connections and create opportunities for you. Who wouldn't want one of these?

Some differences between mentors and sponsors:

- Mentors give their time freely, while sponsors look for a return on the time they invest. A sponsor expects that the time they spend with you will help them in some way.
- Mentors are generally someone who has qualities you'd like to emulate. In many ways, you'd like to learn to

be like them, but that may not be the case with sponsors. They may be very different from you in terms of background, style, and personality. Sponsors often want to support you *because* of your differences. You may be valuable to them because you have skills and qualities they don't possess, like people skills, analytical skills, or tech savvy, or you have access to networks they need.

While the sponsor stands to benefit, there is also a powerful benefit to *you* in having this relationship.

Herminia Ibarra, in a 2019 article in the *Harvard Business Review*, describes it this way: "Sponsorship is a kind of helping relationship in which senior, powerful people use their personal clout to talk up, advocate for, and place a more junior person in a key role. While a mentor is someone who has knowledge and will share it with you, a sponsor is a person who has power and will use it for you."

Wouldn't it be wonderful to have someone who would do that?

Is sponsorship a new thing?

Definitely not. Powerful people have sponsored others since pre-industrial societies. For example, consider the guild relationships of the Middle Ages. Merchants, traders, and artisans provided training for young apprentices (all boys, of course). If they saw real talent, that boy was sponsored for membership in the guild, where he was then given opportunities to work his way up to become a master.

Sponsorship, in modern corporate times, has continued to have more than a touch of the guild, and in many organizations, power has been passed on as a means of repayment of favors from powerful people. (Need I say again that these have historically been mostly men?)

So, while sponsorship has existed, for much of that time it hasn't been available to women.

These days, you'll find that sponsorship is everywhere, and it's for both men and women. Still, studies over the past decade have shown that men are more likely than women to have a sponsor. The Centre for Talent Innovation says that 71 percent of executives have protégées whose gender and race match their own. This can create a sticky situation when most executives are white men.

Because of the unofficial nature of sponsorship, it's hard for organizations to gauge where and when these alliances are in place and what the impact is. Sponsorship is often beneath HR's radar. Some companies have tried to set up formal sponsorship programs, but it's a unique kind of connection, even more nuanced than mentor-mentee relationships. These bonds won't work if they aren't naturally generated and genuinely helpful to both parties.

Does that mean you should just do your job and hope you get lucky? Definitely not. As you'll see, there are plenty of ways to encourage sponsorship. Remember our focus on standing for something, being visible, stepping up, and connecting with many people? These efforts can help you to land the sponsorship that will launch you on your journey.

First, let's take a deeper dive into why this is worth it.

What sponsors can do for you

If you're fortunate enough to have a sponsor, research shows that you're more likely to get promoted and more likely to take on significant responsibilities. Sponsorship can also help you get the resources you need to be successful on a project.

Sylvia Ann Hewlett says that, based on her research with the Center for Talent Innovation, sponsors usually do some or all of these:

- Give valuable advice
- Link their reputation to you and go out on a limb on your behalf
- Act as your champion, convincing others that you deserve a pay increase or a promotion
- Help make it safe for you to take risks

Think about how these actions could potentially change the trajectory of your career.

Do you think you don't have any sponsors? You may want to think again.

Felicity and I reviewed her impressive career path in communications during a coaching session. I'd just introduced the concept of sponsorship and wondered if she had any sponsors. She concluded, with some disappointment, that she couldn't think of any. No one had taken her under their wing, stretched her to take on new opportunities, told her how to get resources, or fought for a promotion for her. She couldn't think of a single example.

And yet, you only had to look at her achievement-filled resume to know that there must have been sponsorship there somewhere. She just hadn't realized it. Felicity had worked with some of the best companies and had spearheaded major com-munity initiatives. She hadn't achieved all that single-handedly. As we talked, she realized that so much of what she'd achieved had come from people getting excited about her creative ini-tiatives and seeing how she operated, and when it was time to make the decision, the right people had backed her.

Felicity's work and initiatives had many, many advocates. And she began to realize that some of those advocates had turned into sponsors who helped her get her initiatives across the finish line.

Sponsorship is not always obvious. When you recognize that someone's your sponsor, you'll want to do what you can to make it a mutually beneficial relationship. And you'll want to reciprocate if you can. Let's start by exploring what they need.

What sponsors need from you

Once you realize that you have one or more sponsors, it's important to treat those relationships with respect and apprecia-tion. The worst thing you can do is take them for granted or act like you'd have achieved the same outcome without their help.

So, what do they need from you? Sponsors need you to:

- Deliver on the commitment they have backed you for.
- Communicate and let them know early if there's a serious risk that you won't have a successful outcome. Remember that it's likely to reflect badly on them if you don't.
- Stay in the loop and let them know if there are issues that might affect them, even issues that might have nothing to do with your work.

- Stay loyal. You need to have their back. In some cases, you may need to offer support when things aren't going well for them.
- Acknowledge them for what they've done on your behalf.

Maybe you already have sponsors

To determine if someone is sponsoring you, ask yourself if someone in your life has done any of the following:

- Helped you see that you're capable of bigger things than you'd previously considered
- Connected you to senior leaders inside your organization
- Asked you to step in for them at a conference they can't attend
- Supported you for an award
- Boosted your visibility in some way
- Provided you with stretch opportunities
- Connected you to clients or customers
- Given you honest, critical feedback about where you need to improve your game
- Suggested that you apply for a role you would never have considered

If someone has done any of these, watch this person carefully. They are probably a sponsor. Thank them for their support. You may want to communicate that you know they have been instrumental in helping you to achieve all that you have. Share your appreciation and acknowledgement.

How to find sponsors

Here's the million-dollar question: how do you get a sponsor? To attract sponsorship, draw on the concepts we've covered in the previous strategies in this book. Be clear about your strengths, stand for something, and be visible to others. You'll need to be courageous and honest in the way you communicate and connect with a diverse group of people. All the work you've done in those earlier strategies is about to pay off.

Here are additional steps that will help you find the people you need.

Step 1: Look at your existing champions who are not yet sponsors.

Good bets are leaders who:

- Are already aware of your skills and strengths
- Stand to benefit from your help
- Have the clout to move you toward your goal

Earlier in this chapter, you identified supporters and advocates. From this group of people, choose someone who could potentially become a sponsor. Invite them to coffee or lunch, thank them for their past support, and ask some questions. Learn from them. Be curious about what they're thinking or working on. Be interested in what they may need from you. The idea is to be able to help them in either small or large ways. This may seem daunting if the person is senior to you, but even the most senior people need good people in their camps.

Step 2: Could your mentor become a sponsor?

YOU MUST BE VISIBLE TO BE SEEN BY POTENTIAL SPONSORS. NO ONE WILL STEP FORWARD TO SPONSOR YOU IF YOU STAY BENEATH THE RADAR, JUST DOING WHAT'S IN YOUR JOB DESCRIPTION AND NO MORE. YOU NEED TO BE OUT THERE, SHOWING WHAT YOU'VE GOT.

If you have a solid mentor relationship, that person may well become a sponsor for you. You've already established trust and confidence. You've listened to them and grown from their support. When an opportunity comes for them to speak up on your behalf, a mentor is very likely to do so, which can suddenly turn into sponsorship. So, if you didn't think it was worth it to find a mentor, think again. If you don't have one, revisit that section in this chapter.

Step 3: Be visible in general.

Visibility is a theme that's been in almost every strategy of this book. That's how important it is. This strategy is no exception.

You must be visible to be seen by potential sponsors. No one will step forward to sponsor you if you stay beneath the radar, just doing what's in your job description and no more. You need to be out there, showing what you've got.

Your visibility through presentations, articles, posts, participation in projects, volunteer activities, and connections will help others see you and make you available for sponsorship.

Step 4: Identify your ideal sponsor.

Watch for the people who have the qualities you need in a sponsor. The ideal sponsor should be someone who can make things happen. In a large firm, they're likely to be two or more levels above you. But in a flatter or smaller firm, they might just be one level above and, even occasionally, at your level.

Here's a same-level example.

> Annie was a highly creative data manager who had developed an innovation team for a growing fintech company. She'd partnered on projects with a product colleague for a couple of years, making his group shine with the help of her team's insights. When her colleague was appointed as the new product VP, she felt left behind and a little bit jealous.
>
> However, it turned out that he hadn't forgotten her. He pointed out to the executive team just how critical her role was to the company's success and persuaded them to create a VP of data role for her. His enthusiastic and well-reasoned support won the day.

Watch out for the wrong kind of sponsor.

Your sponsor has seen you, been impressed by your work, and has helped you in some way. But before you run off with just anyone who shows interest in you, ask yourself a few questions:

- Do you respect this person? Do you trust them?
- Is this person generally held in high regard in your organization, industry, and community?
- Do you feel good having your name associated with this person?

You may think you can't afford to be picky. But in some cases, you need to be. Here's an example from my career:

Geoff had been instrumental in recruiting me to my first big firm consulting role. A partner, he was engaging, smart, and smooth, and he supported me with other partners. I felt lucky— until I began to notice his aberrant behavior, which made me uncomfortable. He drank too much at lunchtime, engaged in inappropriate locker room talk with clients, and displayed a general lack of work ethic. He put his hours on my consulting projects and other consultants' projects, even if he'd done no work on them. In fact, he never even glanced at the work. The longer I looked, the more I realized he didn't do much at all. And I realized that others saw this, too.

I was his protégé, and people knew it. Some of them seemed to be avoiding me. They didn't respect him, so they didn't respect me. I realized that this association wasn't beneficial for me, so I began to spend more time with other partners, seeking their input and advice on my projects and ideas. They gradually took an interest in me, and when the time came, they supported my promotion.

Geoff was, not surprisingly, uncomfortable about what he saw as my defection. I let him know that I was grateful for the support he'd given me and reminded him that it was important for me to work with people across the firm. I treated him with respect, and I didn't criticize him behind his back. Our relationship was no longer close, but it was collegiate.

Step 5: Ask for what you need.

Once you've identified your ideal sponsor, you'll need to find a way to connect. Here are some ways that have worked for my clients.

- Ask for career development advice.
- Ask for a stretch assignment within their line of sight.
- Approach them and suggest collaboration on a project of interest to them, like co-authoring an article.
- Ask for help when you're learning something new. Never, never be afraid to ask for help in a new situation. In their wonderful book *How Women Rise*, Sally Helgesen and Marshall Goldsmith say that women often fail to enlist allies in new roles. They think they must first learn the role. As the authors say, "Women who assume new positions resolve to keep their heads down until they've mastered the details and are confident that they can perform to a certain standard. They want to feel fully prepared before they start reaching out."

However, they point out that this is precisely when you should reach out. You'll get more support. People will be flattered and honored that you want their help, and you'll feel less isolated.

How many sponsors do you need?

If you do all the above, you may find yourself with a real live sponsor, or if you're lucky, a few sponsors. What's the right number? Sylvia Ann Hewlett suggests a "2 + 1" rule. Based on research from the Center for Talent Innovation, she's found that it's helpful to have two sponsors within your organization (one in your area and one in a different department or division) and one outside your organization. If you wonder whether you really need an external sponsor, go back to Strategy 6 and think about the value of external connections. Your career is likely to span decades, and for most people, it doesn't make sense to focus only on the place you are working now.

How to work with your sponsor

Here are some pointers to make your sponsorship relationship successful. Some of these have been referred to previously, but they bear repeating.

- Don't make it all about you. If you've had a mentor before, you may have the idea that you and your career growth needs should be the focus of your conversations. That's not the case here. Once you have a sponsor, you're a team. Your sponsor's needs should be 50 percent of what you discuss when you meet.
- If things aren't going well on your sponsored assignment, talk to your sponsor *before* you get into trouble. If they have advocated for you to work on a project, but things look like they may go south, bring it up early. If you don't deliver, it's a reflection on the person who vouched for you.
- Ask for your sponsor's feedback. They're probably not formally in charge of your work, but they can provide valuable perspectives. If there's something they think you're not getting right, you need to know. Keep them in the loop so they can offer guidance or intervention.
- Deliver more than asked. Okay, this is useful in any role, but when you've been sponsored, it's the perfect

time to bring in your creative juices, problem-solving know-how, and strategic thinking. Share any and all of this with your sponsor and on the job.

- Be thoughtful and considerate. Don't take them for granted. Show gratitude.

In this chapter, you've learned how to gather champions from a variety of sources and how to get the most out of these relationships.

Our final strategy is very different. All the good work, visibility, and success in the world don't mean much if you don't think the work you're doing matters. If you're not doing work you love, how can you find meaning in your work?

RISE WITH WORK THAT MATTERS

"The belief that you can have a meaningful career is the first step to finding one."

—Shawn Achor

INITIALLY, I WASN'T sure whether this chapter should be the first or the last chapter in this book. I put it at the end because, for most of us, finding work that matters is a journey. Rarely do we get it right straight out of the gate—not in our first job, our second, or more. You may end up being decades into your career when you "get" what your purpose is at work. But if you're reading this, either with curiosity or a desire to make a change, now may be the time to explore this existential question: "What kind of work is a labor of love for me?" Because that is work that matters.

The search for meaning is a privilege. Many women (and men) in the workplace struggle to meet the basic needs of their families. Many of them must be content to bring home money to pay the rent and the bills. Maybe that's you. If you're fortunate enough to have an education and to have started a career, you have a huge head start and a much better chance of finding a role that has great meaning and purpose for you. For others, that may not be the case, at least not yet.

Almost none of us are lucky enough to find ultimate meaning in our first job. Most of us aren't even looking for it. Take me, for example.

At seventeen, my first job was cleaning toilets. I scored a much-needed work-study employment opportunity as part of my freshman financial aid package. With no job experience, they started me—literally—at the bottom. I traversed the campus administration buildings, moving quietly from toilet to toilet. I scoured the bowls and scrubbed the porcelain exterior. The fruity aroma of the pink cleanser still lingers in my olfactory memory bank.

I didn't get to clean the whole bathroom. That would have been a promotion. I couldn't even dream of mopping a lobby or dusting an office. What's more, a much faster worker must have performed the time-and-motion studies, as I was given impossibly quick goals for how long I could spend cleaning each toilet. This led to a tendency (at least on my part) to skip the toilets that obviously hadn't been used since I'd wiped them down the day before.

Can I tell you that it did not feel good? I wore a mandatory pink-and-white-striped pinafore and carted around my small, well-used loo mop, fruity cleanser, and bucket. In full regalia,

I passed other students. I passed my professors. And I began dreaming of a better job.

However, a better job, in my mind, didn't need to have more meaning. I just wanted a job that was less embarrassing and boring—and maybe more hygienic. It could be any job that made me feel better about myself. I was at that stage in life (seventeen, remember?) when I thought mostly about myself and very little about others. (Except, of course, I spent quite a bit of time obsessing about what others thought of me.)

I hadn't yet begun to think about meaning at work or about loving my work. And I wouldn't for some time to come.

The sad reality is that much of the world is stuck for their whole lives in (metaphorically speaking) toilet-cleaning jobs. They do their jobs because they have to, not because they want to. They grow numb and lose confidence that they can do more, and they stay there. They may notice that others are passing them by and may feel resentful about that. But they don't realize that they could make it all play out differently.

What about you? You'll never gain the vision, insight, and confidence to go beyond that if you:

- Don't take the time to think about your strengths; instead, focus only on your weaknesses.
- Refuse to work on yourself and explore new paths of growth because you don't believe your work could ever light you up.
- Don't ask for help from others, thinking that you shouldn't need help.

- Stay invisible, thinking, *Why would I want to take the risk of standing out?* You stay under the radar, fearing being seen.
- Say what's expected, not what you really think. You don't ask for what you really want. You don't advocate for yourself.
- Stay isolated and only work with the people you've been assigned to work with. You don't reach out to others who could inspire you, motivate you, help you, and make it more fun to be at work.
- Stay powerless, complaining about your work, problems, and barriers. You don't take the steps to find the power to change.

If the list above describes you, you're in for a disappointing life.

Many people live like that. Many of my clients were at this point when we started our work together. They'd achieved a lot, but there was an emptiness about their work. They asked themselves the meaning-of-life question, "Is that all there is? Just doing the job for the sake of doing the job?"

It is possible to have both meaningful work and good pay. But you first need to know what is meaningful for you. You need to be creative about finding that meaning and finding a way to be paid well for it.

If you've done the exercises in this book, you know your strengths, you've stepped up, and you've found support through connection. Maybe you excel at your job and can see a path to move up. Or you're *not* doing well and can see that you need to move on.

Either way, you may be yearning for a path with more purpose and meaning. You want something more than a good job. You want a job that makes a difference. So, let's explore the world of meaning, purpose, and fulfillment at work.

HOW TO FIND MEANING AT WORK

You may be tempted to just quit your job and look for what you really want to do. While this isn't a move I recommend for most people, in some rare circumstances, it can be the right thing to do, especially if the job you're doing is quietly killing you. I've known several people who've had jobs that were so out of whack that they had complete physical breakdowns. One person woke up unable to walk; another passed out and awakened in an ambulance; another woke up with her face buried in a carpet. I've had clients who've struggled with debilitating work-related depression, who've told me that their work is "sucking the life out of me."

> ... YOU MAY BE YEARNING FOR A PATH WITH MORE PURPOSE AND MEANING. YOU WANT SOMETHING MORE THAN A GOOD JOB. YOU WANT A JOB THAT MAKES A DIFFERENCE.

While many of these people managed to recover and return to work with better boundaries or to find new work that was suited for them, some people don't get that chance. Have you heard of *karoshi*, a Japanese term that literally means "overwork death"? If it were uncommon, they wouldn't have a term for it.

And it's not just in Japan. Burnout is all too real in the West. Ever heard of the stressed-out person who has a heart attack on the job? We've long known that Mondays are the most likely days to have a serious heart attack, which was reinforced by 2023 findings from the British Cardiovascular Society. There's no doubt that toxic workplaces contribute to illnesses, both small and temporary and large and life-threatening.

Don't let it get to that point.

Again, you must own your work life. Your company shouldn't—and doesn't—own you. You are not part of the company's capital. And you aren't a prisoner. You're free to leave whenever you want to. The answer to finding purposeful work might be to leave your job, but if you quit without financial security and have no other way to support yourself, you can create a new cascade of pain and stress for you and your loved ones.

Plenty of my clients came to me feeling that work is joyless and unrewarding. If this is you, there are two possibilities you might want to consider before you jump ship completely. Sometimes, you'll be able to find meaning in the work you have by approaching it differently. You can also look for more meaningful opportunities within your organization. Let's explore each of these.

> ... YOU MUST OWN YOUR WORK LIFE. YOUR COMPANY SHOULDN'T—AND DOESN'T—OWN YOU. YOU ARE NOT PART OF THE COMPANY'S CAPITAL. AND YOU AREN'T A PRISONER.

FIND MEANING IN THE JOB YOU HAVE

Shawn Achor, author of *Big Potential*, says that big potential starts with you, and it's up to you to find meaning in your current position. He asks these questions:

- Are you helping to improve people's lives with your work?
- Are you able to connect with people at a deeper level?

When people feel burned out or bored in their roles, I encourage them to look at what they might not be seeing about their job before they decide to change roles. If changing roles is a knee-jerk reaction, they may find that the next role isn't any better. So, think about what needs to be fixed about your current job to make it more satisfying.

It could be that your job, or the way you do your job, can be changed. Too often, people think there's only one way to perform their role (the way their predecessor performed it or how they've worked in past roles), but that's not usually the case.

These five Rs can help you find meaning in your current role:

- Reframe
- Repurpose
- Reconnect
- Reimagine
- Redefine

Reframe your job

I once interviewed the manager of a factory that made inexpensive, functional, identical bricks. The factory was almost fully automated with only a few employees. And yet, this man showed genuine joy when he told me how much he loved his work. He said, "I love making these bricks so that people will have safety and shelter and can achieve their dreams of owning a home."

To reframe means to find the value in your work that's already there. It doesn't necessarily fix the day-to-day discomfort with your actual role. For that, you might need to repurpose.

Repurpose the work you're already doing

When you repurpose, you find a new use for something that no longer works in its original capacity. One example is using old tires to make freeways in Arizona. This enabled the state to build roads that can withstand the extreme summer heat, have an extended life, and provide a smooth and quiet ride.

But how would you repurpose your job? Maybe the way you work is outdated, or your processes are clunky, or your outputs don't provide much value.

For example, when you joined your organization, your role was "to provide customer data to senior leadership that gives them information to make decisions about whether the product needs to be changed." The role may have seemed joyless because you didn't get to participate in the actual decision-making. You provided data for the sake of providing data, and the interesting part was done by someone else.

So, what could make it more interesting or useful? To find the meaning, you could:

- Ask yourself, "What's the larger purpose behind my role? How does it make a difference? How could I change my role to make a greater difference in terms of customer outcomes?"
- Talk to your stakeholders about how they use the data you provide. What could make it more useful for them?
- Connect in new ways with customers to find real stories behind the data.
- Generate ideas and recommendations with your report.

Using this approach, you could set a new tone for your work and potentially grow your role into something more satisfying. Here's another example:

Adele Scheele, in the introduction to her classic book, Skills for Success, *tells a story about a bright and qualified young woman who found herself in a stultifying clerical job at a small environmental planning firm. Scheele asked her if there was anything about the role she liked, and the woman said she liked searching the newspapers each day for articles that were relevant to the planners who were always on the lookout for potential business opportunities. Unfortunately, as Scheele pointed out, "the best ninety minutes of her day were over before her first coffee break." Scheele encouraged her to save the articles and do some further research by contacting the companies for more information. She then created a Monday morning presentation where she could share these opportunities for new business.*

After her first presentation, the environmental planners (suspecting she could add even more value) asked her to write a project proposal for one of the opportunities. Within two weeks, she had a new position as a proposal writer.

To this young woman's envious friends, it might have looked like she'd had a huge stroke of luck. But it wasn't luck. She'd found a way to add value and to be of greater service to the environmental planners. Most people don't think that way.

If you're just doing your job the way it's always been done, you're almost certainly missing opportunities for more meaning.

Reconnect through service to your stakeholders

It may be time to build important, new connections with your existing stakeholders. Remember Strategy 5, Rise through Authentic Connections, and the four directions of networking? One of those directions was *connection across*, which focused on better connection with your stakeholders. According to the book *Conscious Capitalism* by John Mackey and Raj Sisodia, stakeholders include customers, employees, owners/shareholders, the community, and the environment. Each of these merits your attention.

IF YOU'RE JUST DOING YOUR JOB THE WAY IT'S ALWAYS BEEN DONE, YOU'RE ALMOST CERTAINLY MISSING OPPORTUNITIES FOR MORE MEANING.

Too often, employees focus only on serving their manager because that's who gives feedback on how well they have performed their role and, of course, authorizes salary increases and bonuses.

However, if you only serve your manager, you'll miss opportunities to be of genuine service to your stakeholders. Expanding your view of who you serve can sometimes make all the difference in your success. Let's look more closely at who your most important stakeholders are.

Identify your stakeholders.

"Who am I here to serve in life?" The answer to this question will be different for everyone. If you took a good look at your list of stakeholders in work and life, it might overwhelm you. To make it easier, make a separate list for your personal stakeholders and one for your work stakeholders. Make your list as specific as possible. Avoid catch-all categories like "the world," "the community," or "my business."

> "WHO AM I HERE TO SERVE IN LIFE?" THE ANSWER TO THIS QUESTION WILL BE DIFFERENT FOR EVERYONE.

Your personal stakeholders might include:

- Your life partner
- Your immediate family
- Volunteer organizations
- Your friends
- Your extended family
- The people in your church or other place of worship
- Any community group where you participate or have a key role

- Yourself—this might include how you nourish and replenish yourself mentally, physically, and spiritually

Your work stakeholders might include:

- Your manager
- Your colleagues and peers
- Your team
- The people to whom you provide outputs, so they can get their job done
- The people who provide inputs to you, so you can get your job done
- The people you serve with on committees
- Your customers
- Yourself—this might include the ways you learn and grow at work

Remember that your stakeholders are people, not things, projects, or departments. When you realize that stakeholders are human beings, it's much easier to connect with them. They have names. They have needs. They have homes and families and fears and hopes and hobbies. They have personalities. This makes them more complex, but in a way, it makes the connection so much easier and so much more meaningful and maybe even more fun.

Since they are people, appeal to them as people. It's hard to connect with accounting about whether there are funds for your new idea. It's a little easier to connect with Arthur from accounting, who goes hang-gliding on the weekends, whose daughter just got accepted to college, and who cares about the success of the business and can help you negotiate this challenge.

Notice that you are on both lists. It could be argued that you can't really be your own stakeholder, but if you don't give yourself the same consideration and respect you give others, you could well burn yourself out.

Now that you have this list, narrow it down to the top five to make it more manageable. (Again, I hope you will include yourself on each.) Then, take each of your top five and try out the following questions:

- Do I know their needs? Have I let them know what my needs are?
- How well am I serving each one?
- How do I know I'm right about the questions above? Could I ask them those questions?
- What's the single most important way I could improve my connection with them?

Reconnection can help you find a better sense of purpose, but for some, there's another challenge that can make a profound difference. It involves your imagination.

Reimagine what your job could become

A job description is a piece of paper—or perhaps a screen on a computer. There's nothing permanent or indelible about it. But people stick to doing what's on their job descriptions because they know that's how their success will be measured. In reality, job descriptions are constantly evolving. Sometimes, it happens because a role is eliminated, and the work needs to be folded into someone else's role. Sometimes, a new initiative arises, and someone must take on additional responsibility. Sometimes, it's changed because the person in the role goes way beyond their job description, such as in Paula's case.

When Paula was newly hired in her law firm, she was given a job description that had been written for the new role. Two years later, her original job description was irrelevant. She was frequently asked to speak, collaborate with external groups, write, and create reports. Paula went with what was needed, not what was on the job description, and she performed her role in a way that her manager and the partners in the firm appreciated. She chose not to be limited by her job description and lived in growth mode, doing the job in a way that made a difference rather than sticking to a list of to-dos. Eventually, when she showed her manager the discrepancy in her documented role and her actual role, her job description was rewritten.

No matter what your job description says, there's always the potential to go beyond that. But in most cases, it will be up to you to imagine what the job could be. What does the business need you to be? What contribution do your customers and stakeholders need you to make? What would be the best possible use of your talents and gifts? What if you started to fully bring yourself to work, instead of simply doing what the person before you did?

There's one more way that you can find meaning in your role. You can look at why and how you do your job. This can make all the difference.

Redefine why and how you do what you do

Simon Sinek is well known for his TED talk, "How Great Leaders Inspire Action" (viewed over 60 million times on the TED website). The talk focuses on the need for businesses to grapple with the underlying question of why they are in business. One great example of a company that has done this well is Barry-Wehmiller.

Barry-Wehmiller makes equipment for packaging, paper converting, and corrugating. Among many other paper and packaging products, they make equipment used to manufacture toilet paper rolls. Their factories are mostly in small towns across the USA, and their workforce is highly unionized. For most CEOs, it wouldn't be obvious that their company had a higher purpose that could motivate the people in these factories.

However, Bob Chapman isn't like most CEOs. In the book, *Everybody Matters*, Raj Sisodia and Chapman (now the Chairman of Barry-Wehmiller) explain the company's remarkable journey from a traditional profits-at-any-cost company to becoming all about the people who work in the company. Their guiding principles start with this bold statement: "We measure 'success' by the way we touch the lives of people." The story of how they brought this all to life is shared by Simon Sinek in his bestselling book *Leaders Eat Last* and is documented in detail in Chapman's book.

"But I'm not a CEO," you may say. "I don't have that kind of power." You don't have to be a CEO. You don't even have to work in a conscious business like Barry-Wehmiller to be a conscious leader. You can start where you are. You do that by changing why and how you do what you do.

Let's look at Richard, a manager at an institutional bank where I worked. Richard was able to take a huge pivot without ever leaving his job. He discovered that changing his "why" and his "how" made him more effective and had a bigger impact than he expected.

The essence of Richard's role was to lead a team to make wealthy people wealthier, which is a fine job for someone who's only focused on money, not on purpose. At the time, he came across as an aggressive, competitive, tough guy, so much so that I was a little intimidated by his critical nature and easy dismissal of the soft leadership principles I was advocating.

However, as is so often the case, as Richard began to open up, it became clear that the tough guy image was a work persona he thought he had to maintain to be effective. In his home life, he was a loving husband, a parent of two children, and a person who genuinely cared about other people, including those who worked for him. But he didn't know he could show any of that at work. Like many managers, he'd been taught that to show you care is to show weakness. He didn't know that the opposite was true—that showing he cared would make him a better leader than he'd ever been, a leader people followed because they wanted to rather than because they had to.

Over time, Richard relaxed into his better self. People leadership became his primary function at work. He helped his people, and therefore the business, to be more successful. He got involved in volunteer work for a charity he deeply cared about. He began a cycling group at work and involved his colleagues and his team in races for charity. He continued to do his job well, and he did it with heart.

Gradually, people around him began to relax into themselves, too. Pru, a senior female colleague who'd been known for her aggressive, in-your-face style, began to engage in celebrations of team members' success. She found pleasure in small, anonymous acts of kindness to her colleagues at work.

Jeremy, an executive who worked for Richard, had previously had an intense short-term focus, and he took no prisoners when something went wrong. Jeremy gradually changed his style and eventually started a foundation for social good. Finally, even Richard's manager (who'd been a role model for the previous cutthroat culture) decided he wanted what all these others had experienced and began to make changes to his leadership style only a few years before his retirement.

Because of Richard's transformation, these other people were inspired to find meaning in and around their work, and their impact spread in the business and the community. The business did better by doing good. They made a difference.

> MANY PEOPLE ASSUME THAT IF THEY AREN'T HAPPY IN THEIR ROLE, THEY NEED TO MOVE TO ANOTHER ORGANIZATION.... BUT IS THERE ANOTHER PART OF THE BUSINESS WHERE YOU MIGHT THRIVE?

Finding meaning in your current role can happen at any time in your career.

However, if you've tried to reframe, repurpose, reconnect, reimagine, and redefine in your current role and none of them have helped you find meaning, you may be in a serious mismatch in your current job. Even so, it's still not time to jump ship. First, let's look at other possibilities within the broader business.

LOOK FOR MEANING IN OTHER PARTS OF YOUR ORGANIZATION

Many people assume that if they aren't happy in their role (for any reason), they need to move to another organization. If you feel this way, first look at one more possibility: is there another part of the business where you might thrive?

Here are a few reasons you might want to consider this option.

- It's an easier way to make a transition. An external job search is a difficult and challenging process. You won't be able to see deep inside a company that's new to you, so you don't know what's hiding in its dark corners that aren't open to public view. You can be more confident when you navigate a search for internal roles. You know the people, culture, and processes.
- You're likely to have more connections and access to others in the organization. Usually, even people you don't know will be willing to talk to you. With luck, you'll have access to others who work in an area that interests you.
- You won't lose the perks that go with length of service. You may want to try the following approaches.

You can look for a more aligned culture within your business

While most businesses try hard to create one culture for the whole organization, few successfully achieve that. Every leader throughout the entity puts their imprint on their team's culture, for better or for worse.

Do you remember Bronte from Strategy 2, who came across a new team that would focus on customer experience? This perfectly aligned with her values and her authentic desire to create and implement change programs that were based on the customer's perspective. She was able to talk to the manager about his vision for the team and found great alignment both in terms of what the new team would do and how they would do it. While her new role was similar to one she had previously held, the culture was very different than the one she had worked in, and it made Bronte feel excited and alive.

Somewhere in your business, there might be a leader who is creating a "village" like Bronte's new manager, an environment that will be fulfilling for you. It's worth taking the time to look for that.

You can look for a new type of role

If you want to get a completely different type of role than the one you're currently in, it will be easier to find it in your current organization, where you're a known quantity.

There are many types of roles you might be able to transition to, and you may find opportunities in both small and large businesses.

Marla was in her twenties and had just graduated with a marketing degree. After college, she wasn't able to find a role that used her degree, so she worked as a sales clerk in a sporting goods store. After a long search, she landed an entry-level role in digital marketing for a small (ten-employee), successful startup that sold camping supplies. She wrote content for social media blasts, but to her surprise, she didn't enjoy that type of writing. She realized that one of her biggest strengths was working with people. As the company grew, it needed an HR manager, and Marla put her hand up. The company agreed to pay for additional training to help her be successful in the role. Suddenly, her talents began to shine through, and Marla ultimately forged a successful career in HR.

There are even more opportunities to pivot in a larger organization:

At fifty, Daniele had executed several successful turnarounds in a large technology company. She was now the head of her division and was widely recognized as a strong people leader. Still, after so many years, Daniele felt burned out from the constant adrenaline pumping and do-or-die environment of turnarounds. She wondered how much positive impact she'd had in her career. Yes, she'd enjoyed it, but she didn't love it. And she wanted more meaning.

Through the corporate grapevine, she heard about a new nonprofit foundation that the company was starting. She was enthusiastic about the foundation's vision. They aimed to make real change in the lives of thousands of others by providing fellowships for college graduates with game-changing, viable proposals for projects that would build the region and meet social needs. They were looking for a hands-on CEO who would bring that vision to life.

Even though she had no nonprofit experience, the board knew that she could develop a strategy that would make their vision come to life. Her past successes and strong support from other senior leaders helped her land this role.

Had Daniele applied for a CEO role at an external non-profit, she almost certainly would not have been considered. Nonprofit leadership generally requires a different set of skills than leading a business turnaround. However, within her company, Daniele was trusted. She had the skills, perspectives, and willingness to learn that she needed for the job (plus the ability to work with the company's board, which was invaluable).

Daniele spent the last ten years of her career creating the foundation's impact at a national level, and she built a successful, strong team that could keep the work going for decades to come.

How to look for internal opportunities

If you work in a large company, jobs are typically posted as they become available. Most people look for a job that interests them. But you don't need to wait for that. You can be proactive.

First, go back to the "What I want to stand for at work" statement you developed as part of Strategy 2. With that clarity, you can begin to look around your business. When you see an area that interests you, dig deeper. Make sure you understand the structure, workflows, and responsibilities. If you work in a small business, this should be easily available. If you're in a large business, get the most detailed organizational structure you can find.

Now, it's time for some deeper research. As much as possible, gather information on any parts of the business that interest you because of what they do.

The next part of your research involves conducting informational interviews with individuals who work there (or have worked there in the past). They can help you understand both what they do and how they do it. These interviews are a golden opportunity. You aren't there to ask for a job; you're on a quest to learn and understand more about this part of the business. This can reduce your stress level in the conversation. Whatever comes out of it, it will be a valuable exercise. Even if you learn that you aren't interested in this area, you've learned something important. And you have a connection you didn't have before.

How to land and conduct a great informational interview

If you already know someone in the part of the business you want to explore, that's a great start. If not, try to find a colleague who can connect you with someone in that area. You can even use LinkedIn to find out who's connected with the people you need to know. If you don't get anywhere with that, you can always take the cold call approach and connect with a person you can see on the organizational chart. Here are some tips for connecting:

- Approach them with a friendly email. Here's one you can adapt: "I'm x, and I work in y. I'd love to learn about your (division, team, project), what you do, and how it all works. I'm not looking to change my job now, but I would like to explore options with the future in mind. Could we have coffee or, if it works better for you, a short online meeting? It would be so helpful to have your knowledge and perspective." Most people will be willing to share with you over a coffee break or a fifteen- to thirty-minute online connection.
- Be prepared for the meeting. Learn as much as you can about the area to ensure your questions are relevant.

No one wants to explain things that you could have found on the company website. And your communication needs to be efficient because you probably won't have a lot of time.

- Show interest in the person. How long have they worked there? What do they do? What do they like most about their work? Is there anything they don't like?
- Be prepared to talk briefly about yourself, but avoid self-promotion. Make this about them, not you. You can also tell them why you're interested in learning about their area. You're likely to be more relaxed because you know this isn't a job interview.
- Thank them after the meeting, either with a sincere email, text, or note.
- Finally, don't be discouraged if your first informational interview isn't perfect. You'll get better at this with practice.

If you think you might like to work there

Once you've done your research and you have an idea about where you might like to work, you can start to watch for opportunities. Those you had informational interviews with might now be your allies and advocates. When you reach this point, you'll likely need to have a conversation with your manager. Most managers expect this from their employees if they're considering making a change.

YOU'VE NOW EXPLORED MANY OPTIONS to find opportunities and support within your company. But what if this still doesn't work? As a coach, I can tell you that this approach works about 90 percent of the time for my clients. However, about one person in ten still feels that they will need to leave their company to find fulfilment in their work.

WHEN YOU KNOW YOU NEED TO LEAVE

If there's a serious mismatch between you and your organization, you may need to look for work in a different business or industry, or in some cases, you might decide you want to work for yourself.

So, how do you do that? It's probably not going to be easy to walk away unless you have a substantial nest egg. If you don't, you can consider the following options. If your current work situation is desperately bad and you're at the end of your rope, there are actions you can take while you look for a new role.

1. Take steps to make work *work* for you in the short term. You might be able to:

    - Set clear boundaries. Decide what hours you will work and say no to requests that take you outside that zone. If applicable, you can cite health reasons, family reasons, or anything else that is true and will help you to say no with firmness. Your manager may not like it, but often, you can set better boundaries than you have in the past.
    - Work from home, at least some of the time. Sometimes, stepping away from the environment can help alleviate some of the pressure.

- Cut your hours. Take an inventory of how much you need to earn to make ends meet. Could you economize and live on less for a while? There are blogs, books, and apps that can help you slim down your financial burden. If you find that you can live on less, you could talk to your manager or HR about part-time work as an option.
- Consider contract work. You may be able to get a contract elsewhere, either part-time or temporary, that will cover your costs while you look for the role you want.

2. Create an exit plan.

- Give yourself a deadline to get everything lined up so you can depart responsibly. Be sure to have your paperwork, systems, and relationships in order and be prepared to do a thorough handover. You don't want to leave a mess or leave your manager in the lurch. That could come back to haunt you.
- Be clear about what you want to do next. This might be a good time to consider hiring a career coach or working with a close friend. You can tap into the exercises in Strategies 1 and 2 to use your strengths and values.

Where should you look? What should you do to find that new, better workplace? There are several options:

- Same industry, same type of work, different employer
- Different industry, same type of work
- Different industry, different type of work
- Starting your own business

Let's explore these here.

Same industry, same type of work, different employer

This may be the easiest transition for you to make if you believe the mismatch is with your company, rather than your industry.

> Helen was a forty-something researcher in a large pharmaceutical company. Recently divorced and a mother of two, she found herself the sole breadwinner for her young family. Armed with a PhD, she'd always given her all to her work. Her love for learning and her passion for medical interventions that made a difference made her work feel meaningful. She'd worked for the same company for many years, but then a change in leadership brought new expectations. Suddenly, she was asked to take on responsibilities that felt more bureaucratic than passionate. With little time now for true innovation, combined with a sense that she needed to be there for her children, she became anxious about the future. She juggled it all (barely) and found herself awake and anxious in the night. She knew this couldn't go on.
>
> Helen decided it was time to explore other opportunities in her field, and she moved to another pharmaceutical company, one that seemed more focused on contributing to great patient outcomes. She was able to get a role that aligned more with her values and offered flexibility to work from home, which was so important at this crucial time in the lives of her family.

Helen managed to make it work without putting her family at risk in the process. She is still at the new company, feeling very loyal and grateful for her outcome.

Different industry, same type of work

Rather than jumping into a different type of work, you might want to change your industry. This is a classic solution for many attorneys who find the pressures of working in a law firm (often with an intense focus on billable hours and selling) aren't for them. Rather than changing to a non-legal career, many choose to work as in-house attorneys for organizations.

It's worth checking to see if your industry is at the root of your ongoing frustration, as in Leticia's case below.

Leticia, pale and slender, came to my office with an unusual client complaint. Many of my clients are frustrated with their jobs, but Leticia's job seemed to literally be making her sick. She worked in a senior finance role for a government department. She liked her manager and the people she worked with, but she struggled frequently with migraine headaches and fatigue. Most of the time, she could power through at work, but she missed a lot of work due to illness. At home, she worked hard to be the wife and mother she wanted to be. She'd been to many doctors who ran tests and were unable to find a diagnosis.

Fortunately, I remembered a previous client who'd told me his wife's story, which sounded remarkably like Leticia's. At one point, his wife had been so weak that she was unable to get out of bed. They'd spent years seeking a diagnosis. When I contacted him, he said that his wife had fully recovered, and he credited the approaches of an integrative medicine physician she'd ultimately seen. I gave Leticia this doctor's phone number so she could find out if this approach might help.

Desperate for relief, Leticia went to see him. He told her that, at that time, there were no definitive tests or clear diagnoses for what she had, but he'd seen the condition many times. The medication he prescribed helped, but the doctor thought that wasn't enough. She needed to engage in activities that would help her maintain a more consistent, even state in her life. She took up yoga and began to slow down. Her husband and children helped more at home.

While that helped, Leticia realized that she still felt dread and stress about her work. As we explored this, she realized that she wanted to do work that felt more purposeful. She began exploring finance positions in nonprofit organizations she admired. They didn't pay as much, but she and her husband felt that their family could manage if she made the change. When we finished our engagement, Leticia was happy, loved her yoga and her work, and was able to go off the medication (and the work treadmill) she'd been on.

Different industry, different type of work

This one may be the biggest challenge of all. Prospective employers usually like to see a sure thing, even before you score an interview. Changing your industry and changing the kind of work you do is a massive stretch, but occasionally, it works, as in Kelsey's case. However, it may require help and influence from someone who believes in you.

Kelsey had previously worked as a producer on a television show. When she moved to a new city, she found that the market for producers was incredibly tight, and she was unable to find a job in her field. Desperate by this point to find any job, she spoke to a family friend who was a senior manager in a bank. Through him, she landed a role in change management for the bank. She was successful, but to get to the starting gate for her new career, she needed someone with influence to see that the skills she'd used in her previous role would be useful to the bank—and she needed him to vouch for her. Fortunately, she loved her job in the bank. When I checked in with her on LinkedIn, I saw that she'd received her third promotion since she changed her career.

Start your own business

Many books and articles have been written on how to leave organizational life to start your own business. That's not the topic of this book, and if you find yourself fantasizing about this option, I encourage you to use the many resources available. In addition to what has been written, many communities offer resources for aspiring entrepreneurs.

Here's the path I took many years ago, when I found myself facing the possibility of becoming a partner at my consulting firm. I looked around me at the other partners and decided it wasn't for me.

There were costs and benefits to starting my own business. Looking back at the challenges I've faced, I'm not entirely certain that I would do it again. I didn't consider myself an entrepreneur; in my view, you need to have a tangible product to be a genuine entrepreneur. And I wasn't a startup. I was simply a self-employed consultant.

Here are the reasons why I decided to go out on my own. Everyone is different. These are probably not your reasons, and they may not be the best reasons. But they were mine.

- **Autonomy:** I didn't have a huge drive to be self-employed, but I did have a massive desire to be independent and to call my own shots. I'd found that in a large consulting firm, I didn't have much choice about the work I did. I could go out and find new clients, but if I wasn't successful at that (and in the early days, I wasn't), I had to do whatever work I was assigned. It was often work I didn't feel was inspiring or enjoyable. Sometimes, the work even clashed with my values. I longed to be able to say no to the occasional consulting assignment. However, the partner I worked for made it clear to me that this wasn't an option when those assignments came with a lot of billable hours.

- **A desire to have an impact:** I felt frustrated by how frequently our clients didn't implement the projects I'd worked on. I suspected that certain projects had been commissioned solely to spend the money allocated before the end of the financial year. When that happened, I was gutted. Much of the work we did was great, and I didn't want it to rot on a shelf in a closet somewhere.

- **Enjoying the clients:** I also wanted to work with people I liked and respected. When you work for a big consulting firm, you don't get to choose your clients. When you're independent and you work hard and market your services to people you like and respect, that's generally where the work will come from.

- **Flexibility:** I wanted to be in charge of my schedule at a time when no employers offered flexibility, and "working from home" always was said with a smirk and air quotes. The only way I could have flexible hours was to be my own boss.

Notice what's missing from the list above. I didn't start my own business to make a lot of money. As most independent consultants will attest, there are far better ways to get rich than a startup, self-managed consulting business.

Some tips if you decide you want to be self-employed

If you are one of the people who want to make this move, here are a few pieces of advice from me.

- **Keep your new business close to what you know well.** I know too many people who have been highly successful in specialist areas and then stepped out because they thought they had broader expertise than they actually had. You won't magically be able to do things you've never done, and learning how to do them takes time. If you don't know how to do something, learn how, or find someone experienced to partner with you.
- **Keep a good relationship with the organization you leave**. Many newly self-employed people keep afloat as contractors with their former employers while they're waiting for their business to kick in. This can really work to your benefit.
- **Become skilled at marketing your services.** In most cases, the work doesn't just magically appear when you let people know you have a startup business or consulting practice. (Sorry, we all had that fantasy.) If you're a coach, the International Coach Federation offers many, many classes in marketing. And there are

small business marketing books and classes available. Note: many people will flood your inbox or LinkedIn profile with offers to help you market yourself. Check their credentials. Even better, check their references. I discovered some bad players out there that cost me thousands of dollars when I could least afford it.

- **Learn to live on as little as possible for the time being.** It may take a while before your business generates an income that's as high as your previous income.
- **Be prepared to pay for everything yourself.** That includes insurance, gyms, marketing, client lunches, etc.
- **Learn to be a good boss to yourself.** Don't be your own taskmaster. This is a lesson I'm still learning.

As this final strategy concludes, I want to circle back to the beginning to make this clear:

The meaning you are seeking is in you already; let it reveal itself.
It's time to find a way for your work to align with your soul.
Listen to the wisdom that is in you. It's there.
You deserve to do work that you love. It may be closer than you can imagine.

CONCLUSION

I F YOU'RE A parent, you probably remember going to parent-teacher interviews when your children were small. I remember that it seemed, at times, like the teacher had so much power to change the entire future of my child.

Will this teacher see her love of reading, his ability to make everyone laugh right at the perfect moment? Will this teacher appreciate the enthusiasm, the creativity, the artistic talent, the love for animals, or the ability to run without stopping? Will this teacher see that my child is special in the ways that I already know about and even identify some that I'm not aware of?

Or will they try to make every child conform so the classroom is easier to manage? Will joy and fun be relegated to recess? Will they force the progress in academics to move at the same rate for all, rather than in alignment with an individual child's readiness? Will each child be a test score, a number at the end of the year?

As a parent, I know that every child is special with something wonderful waiting to be unlocked. And, having gone through the system with two children, I know that most will only come across a handful of teachers who are willing to see the wonder or find the key.

What about you? While I know that you are a grown-ass adult, I also know you aren't finished with your growth, not finished finding the gifts you can bring to the work you do, and not finished unlocking the ways you are special.

As I wrote the above, I thought about that word "special" and realized that, with a little massaging, it forms an acronym for the seven strategies we covered in this book. I haven't always been a fan of acronyms, but I know from working with my clients that they can be helpful, often making principles and steps easier to remember. (Who didn't try to come up with good acronyms when cramming for finals?)

There are a lot of ideas in this book, and I hope they have helped. I don't want you to just read it, put it away, and forget about these ideas. I want you to remember the ones that resonate for you. I want you to remember the ideas that are going to unlock your specialness.

Here's the acronym. Write the word SPECIAL at the top of your journal page or your daily to-do list. Or just think about it at the beginning of your day. By doing that, you'll remember what we covered in this book.

Strengths	Know them. Live them.
Purpose	Find your purpose by knowing what you want to stand for at work.
Exposure	Be visible. Be seen. Put yourself out there in whatever way works best for you.
Courage	Step up. Open up. Speak up. Every day. This needs constant practice.

Intentional Connection	Constantly grow your connections and make them authentic and genuine.
Allies/Champions	Find the team of people you can turn to who will help you grow.
Love your work	Do work that matters to you. Find meaning in your work. Don't settle for less.

You don't need a teacher or boss to fix your career. You are now fully equipped to re-launch your career so it has meaning, purpose, and joy. And you know what you need to do to get there.

I hope this book has helped you to ask (and answer) the questions that will help you rise in your current role and future roles. I want you to be fulfilled and to have an amazing career. And remember my secret agenda for writing this book (for those who may have missed it in the introduction) is that we need you at the top.

We need you to move through the "messy middle" and into senior levels of leadership in your organization.

We need you to be part of the team that makes the bold, courageous, people-focused decisions for the future.

We need you to create the sort of workplace where you can thrive. Where everyone can thrive.

We need you to lead with love and purpose.

We need you to *Rise Like a Woman*.

There's no time to waste.

APPENDIX 1: EXERCISES, ACTIVITIES, AND QUESTIONS FOR EACH STRATEGY

For ease of review, I've put most of the exercises from the book in one place.

Strategy 1: Rise Through Your Strengths

- [ ] Complete the VIA Strengths Survey (www.viacharacter.org).
- [ ] Do the Peak Achievements by Decades exercise from Strategy 1.
- [ ] Using the survey and/or the Peak Achievements Exercise, what do you see as your top five strengths?
- [ ] Ask yourself: "How can I use each of these strengths more in my work?"

Strategy 2: Rise Because You Stand for Something

Take some time to come up with a list of your most important values using:

- ☐ An online values list like this one from Brené Brown:
  - o www.brenebrown.com/resources/ dare-to-lead-list-of-values, or
- ☐ A values instrument like this one from the Barrett Values Centre:
  - o www.valuescentre.com/pva
- ☐ Narrow your list to five core values.
- ☐ To identify your passions, explore:
  - o What's a challenge that always makes you feel excited?
  - o What, over the years, has made you happiest at work?
  - o What idea for your workplace really lights you up?
- ☐ Now integrate your top five strengths, your five core values, and the things you are passionate about or deeply interested in at work. What do they say to you about what you want to stand for at work?
- ☐ Draft a personal statement of *what you want to stand for*. Keep it simple. Check on the following: is the personal statement easy to remember? Does it feel authentic? Is it a statement you can apply in practical ways at work?
- ☐ Keep going until it feels right. It will evolve over time (as you grow and change).
- ☐ Share it with someone you trust (a friend, colleague, or coach) for validation.

Strategy 3: Rise and Be Seen

Before kicking off your visibility plan, you need to make sure you're currently delivering what is expected. Ask these questions of your manager, key stakeholders, or both:

- ☐ Am I focused on the right priorities?
- ☐ Am I achieving what's expected?
- ☐ What would you like more of from me right now?

Once you are confident that your performance and delivery are on-track, pick two or three visibility actions below to work on.

- ☐ Speak up in meetings
- ☐ Get involved with stakeholders
- ☐ Speak in front of groups
- ☐ Participate in an expert panel
- ☐ Write articles
- ☐ Use LinkedIn
- ☐ Use your organization's in-house social media platform
- ☐ Teach what you know
- ☐ Create an event or gathering
- ☐ Join an employee resource group
- ☐ Write a paper on a problem you could help resolve, then share it

To help you stay motivated and to continue stretching yourself, focus on actions that are enjoyable for you.

Strategy 4: Rise with Courage

There are three important ways to show courage at work.

- ☐ Step up – Put your hand up to help and support in new ways.
- ☐ Open up – Be your authentic self at work. Let people know you.
- ☐ Speak up – Raise the hard issues others may be avoiding.

All three of these require the skill of having courageous conversations. Below is a checklist of how to prepare for and have those conversations.

Checklist for Having Courageous Conversations

Parts 1-3: Prepare for the Conversation

Before you decide to have the conversation, ask yourself:

- ☐ What is the *real* conversation you need to have? Stay with this! It's often not what you think at first.
- ☐ What will happen if you don't have the conversation?

Prepare yourself. Ask:

- ☐ Do you have the facts? Are you sure they are facts and not opinions?
- ☐ What's your "story" around those facts (how you've made sense of them)?

☐ Have you imagined how the other person's story might be different?

☐ What's your intent? Is it clean? If it's not, what can you do to get it clean before you set up the conversation?

Prepare to listen to the other person: What do you want or need to know that only they can tell you? What are you curious about? What might they say that could trigger an overreaction from you? How will you stay calm no matter what they say?

Set the stage for success. Check in with these questions:

☐ When should you set up the conversation?

☐ Do you have a private place to meet?

☐ How much time will you need for the conversation?

Part 4: Have the Conversation (Opening and Listening)

The Opening statement

Craft your opening statement carefully, keeping it under two minutes. Explore the following:

☐ Does your opening statement reflect your (clean) intent?

☐ Does it include the facts pertinent to the situation? Are you likely to agree on the facts?

☐ Have you shared how you have made sense of the facts and acknowledged that this is *your* story?

☐ Have you acknowledged any role you have played in the problem with an apology if appropriate?

☐ Will this statement create an environment in which it is safe for the other person(s) to respond?

Listening

Share the opening statement for two minutes, then invite the other person's response. When you are listening, remember to:

- ☐ Focus your attention on what they are saying. Paraphrase what they have said to make sure you have understood.
- ☐ Watch your body language. Make eye contact, lean in, and nod when you agree.
- ☐ Encourage them to continue until they have said all they need/want to say.
- ☐ If they tell you they have struggled, let them know you have heard them and that you care.
- ☐ If they try to immediately suggest a solution, acknowledge that! And remind them that you're still in listening mode. Solutions come next.
- ☐ Before you move to the next stage in the conversation, summarize what you've heard and check on shared understanding.

Part 5: Explore Solutions, Actions and Follow Through

- ☐ Check in to see if you need a break before moving on to explore options for solutions. If so, agree on when to reconvene (make it as soon as possible).
- ☐ Continue to listen if they've thought of more they want to share.
- ☐ Share your own thoughts, feedback, and suggestions. Refer to the previous conversation and the points they made.

- [ ] Go back and forth in the dance of exploration and consider possible solutions as long as needed.
- [ ] Agree on the actions you will take. What are your actions? What are theirs? When will you take those actions?
- [ ] Put this in writing and share it with the other person. Check: did you get it right?
- [ ] How will you follow through?

Strategy 5: Rise Through Intentional Connection

Your capacity for connection

Think about your preferred connection style, which may change depending upon your life's circumstances.

- [ ] Where are you on the introversion/extraversion scale? This may affect the kind of connection you want.
- [ ] How much time do you have available for connection? If you're a very busy person, you'll need to be extra-intentional when you make connection commitments.

The four directions of connection

Which of the four directions of connection is most important to you right now? Why? With whom?

- [ ] Connection *within* your business unit
- [ ] Connection *across* to stakeholders or people in other business units

- ☐ Connection *up* to more senior people
- ☐ Connection *out* of the organization: professional associations, alumni associations, charities, community associations, conferences, social media, etc.

Even if they **all** seem important, it's challenging to do everything at once. For most people, it works best to ease into this work, so pick one or two to work on.

Tracking to maintain relationships

How will you track your connections?
You can...

- ☐ Set up a file on your computer
- ☐ Keep a separate notebook for connections, or
- ☐ Use an app

Make the tracking system as simple as possible so you'll actually use it! Consistency wins the day.

Strategy 6: Rise Through Allies and Champions

Role Models

- ☐ Who might you look to as a role model?
- ☐ Who can you learn from, even if you don't know the person?

Accountability Partners

- ☐ Who do you know who would be willing to hold you accountable on a regular basis?
- ☐ Who won't let you off the hook?
- ☐ Is there a way you can reciprocate? Do they want to be held accountable for a goal?
- ☐ How often do you want to connect and support each other?

Advocates

- ☐ Who has advocated for you in the past?
- ☐ Is there someone you would like to have as an advocate on an idea, a vision, or a project?
- ☐ What sort of advocacy do you need from them? What's one action that would help: a written recommendation, a word with someone they know well, or a resource you need?
- ☐ Ask them. Let them know how much their advocacy would mean.

Mentors

- ☐ Identify someone you know or have met who you'd like to have as a mentor.
- ☐ Craft an email. Ask them if they would consider mentoring you. Explain what qualities you see in them that would make them a great mentor for you, and what you would like to learn from them.

☐ If they agree to meet, set up a coffee or lunch (you're buying!), and work through how both would like the relationship to work. This might include when to meet and your role in setting up questions for them.

Coaches

☐ Check to see if your company provides coaching or will fund your coaching.
☐ Ask around. Who has had a coach, and what did they get from coaching? Would they recommend their coach?

Sponsors

☐ Ask yourself, "Have I had a sponsor in the past, and what did they do for me?" You might want to go back and thank them.
☐ If you realize that someone is sponsoring you now, acknowledge them and see if there is a way to build the relationship so it's beneficial for them.
☐ If you realize you've never had a sponsor:
 o Make a list of what you could do to make others want to sponsor you (Hint: the actions in the previous strategies will make you much more sponsorable!)
 o List the actions you want to take. Pick one and put it into play.

Strategy 7: Rise with Work that Matters

Reflection questions

- ☐ Who do you know who's doing meaningful work? What makes it meaningful?
- ☐ What have you loved—really loved—doing in the past?
- ☐ Albert Schweitzer said, "I don't know what your destiny will be, but one thing I know: the only ones among you who will be really happy are those who have sought and found how to serve." Who do you want to serve? How can you best serve?
- ☐ What do you know that others might need to know? Can you teach it? Would that feel meaningful to you?
- ☐ How can you make life a richer, better experience for others (customers, clients, the general public)?
- ☐ What volunteer work could you do through your organization that would add meaning for you?

The Five Rs: Could you apply any of these?

- ☐ Reframe: How could you reframe the way you think about your role to see the inherent meaning in it?
- ☐ Repurpose: How can you approach your role differently to give it greater meaning?
- ☐ Reconnect: Who are your most important stakeholders? What do they need? How could you improve those relationships?

- ☐ Reimagine: If you could reimagine your role, perhaps by changing your job description, how would that look?
- ☐ Redefine: How can you adapt your role to become closer to what you'd like it to be?

Is it possible find greater meaning in a different part of the company you currently work for?

- ☐ Study the organizational structure. Is there an area there that could be more meaningful for you?
- ☐ If so, who could you speak with to learn more? How can you get the information you need?

If you decide that you need to leave your organization to find meaning

- ☐ How can you prepare for this and do it in a well-thought-out, responsible way—responsible to your employer, responsible to your manager, responsible to your team, and responsible to yourself and your family?
- ☐ Where will you look externally—a different industry, a different employer, or a different type of work?
- ☐ Do you want to start a business? Are you in a position to do that? What do you need to do to make it happen? What resources can you tap into?

APPENDIX 2: BOOKS, ARTICLES, LINKS, AND RESOURCES

Introduction

Perez, Caroline Criado. 2019. *Invisible Women: Data Bias in a World Designed for Men.* New York: Abrams Press.

Mohr, Tara. 2015. *Playing Big: Practical Wisdom for Women Who Want to Speak Up, Create, and Lead.* New York: Avery (Penguin Publishing Group).

Strategy 1: Rise Through Your Strengths

Grant, Adam. "Women Know Exactly What They're Doing When They Use 'Weak Language.'" *The New York Times,* July 31, 2023. www.nytimes.com/2023/07/31/opinion/women-weak-language.html.

VIA Character Strengths Survey.
www.viacharacter.org/survey

Zenger, John H., and Joseph Folkman. 2009. *The Extraordinary Leader: Turning Good Managers into Great Leaders.* 2nd ed. New York: McGraw-Hill.

Helgesen, Sally, and Marshall Goldsmith. 2018. *How Women Rise: Break the 12 Habits Holding You Back From Your Next Raise, Promotion, or Job*. New York: Hachette Books.

Strategy 2: Rise Because You Stand for Something

Cialdini, Robert B. 2021. *Influence: The Psychology of Persuasion*. Revised ed. New York: Harper Business.

Brown, Brené. 2018. *Dare to Lead: Brave Work. Tough Conversations. Whole Hearts*. New York: Random House. www.brenebrown.com/resources/living-into-our-values/

Barrett Values Centre Personal Values Assessment: www.valuescentre.com/pva

"How we lead: conversations with Ken Blanchard", 2019: www.howwelead.org

Strategy 3: Rise and be Seen

Frei, Frances. 2018. "How to Build (and Rebuild) Trust." TED2018, April. Video, 15:17. www.ted.com/talks/frances_frei_how_to_build_and_rebuild_trust.

Strategy 4: Rise with Courage

Patterson, Kerry, Joseph Grenny, Ron McMillan, Al Switzler, and Emily Gregory. 2022. *Crucial Conversations: Tools for Talking when Stakes are High*. 3rd ed. New York: McGraw-Hill.

Bushe, Gervase R. 2009. *Clear Leadership: Sustaining Real Collaboration and Partnership at Work*. Rev. ed. Boston: Davies-Black.

Sinek, Simon. 2017. *Leaders Eat Last: Why Some Teams Pull Together and Others Don't*. New York: Portfolio.

Scott, Susan. 2004. *Fierce Conversations: Achieving Success at Work and in Life One Conversation at a Time*. New York: Berkley.

Strategy 5: Rise with Authentic Connection

Granovetter, Mark S. 1973. "The Strength of Weak Ties." *American Journal of Sociology* 78 (6): 1360–1380.

Grant, A. M. (2013). "Rethinking the Extraverted Sales Ideal: The Ambivert Advantage." *Psychological Science*, 24(6), 1024–1030.

Whitmore, John. 2017. *Coaching for Performance: The Principles and Practice of Coaching and Leadership*. 5th ed. London: Nicholas Brealey Publishing.

Ferrazzi, Keith, and Tahl Raz. 2014. *Never Eat Alone: And Other Secrets to Success, One Relationship at a Time*. Expanded and Updated ed. New York: Crown Currency.

Strategy 6: Rise Through Allies and Champions

Nooyi, Indra. 2021. *My Life in Full: Work, Family, and Our Future*. New York: Portfolio.

Sisodia, Rajendra, David B. Wolfe, and Jagdish N. Sheth. 2014. *Firms of Endearment: How World-Class Companies Profit from Passion and Purpose.* 2nd ed. Upper Saddle River, NJ: Pearson FT Press.

C.J. Hayden's "Get it Written Day," www.cjhayden.com/get-it-written-day/

Mohr, Tara. 2015. *Playing Big: Practical Wisdom for Women Who Want to Speak Up, Create, and Lead.* New York: Avery (Penguin Publishing Group).

Cialdini, Robert B. 2021. *Influence: The Psychology of Persuasion.* Revised ed. New York: Harper Business.

Hewlett, Sylvia Ann. 2013. *Forget a Mentor, Find a Sponsor: The New Way to Fast-Track Your Career.* Boston: Harvard Business Review Press.

Ibarra, Herminia. 2019. "A Lack of Sponsorship Is Keeping Women from Advancing into Leadership." *Harvard Business Review,* August 19. hbr.org/2019/08/a-lack-of-sponsorship-is-keeping-women-from-advancing-into-leadership.

Helgesen, Sally, and Marshall Goldsmith. 2018. *How Women Rise: Break the 12 Habits Holding You Back from Your Next Raise, Promotion, or Job.* New York: Hachette Books.

Strategy 7: Rise with Work That Matters

Achor, Shawn. 2018. *Big Potential: How Transforming the Pursuit of Success Raises Our Achievement, Happiness, and Well-Being.* New York: Crown Publishing Group.

Mackey, John, and Rajendra Sisodia. 2013. *Conscious Capitalism: Liberating the Heroic Spirit of Business.* Boston, MA: Harvard Business Review Press.

Scheele, Adele M. 1981. *Skills for Success.* New York: Ballantine Books.

Sinek, Simon. 2009. "How Great Leaders Inspire Action." Filmed September 2009 at TEDxPuget Sound. Video, 18:04. TED. www.ted.com/talks/simon_sinek_how_great_leaders_inspire_action.

Chapman, Bob, and Raj Sisodia. 2015. *Everybody Matters: The Extraordinary Power of Caring for Your People Like Family.* New York: Portfolio/Penguin.

ACKNOWLEDGMENTS

USUALLY, AT THIS point, authors thank friends, family, coworkers, and colleagues for reading early drafts, pointing them in the right direction, helping them be better writers, and so on. However, for this book, there is only one person to thank for all of this, and that is my book coach, Nancy Erickson. I chose her because she could do all these things—and she has done them so well.

However, there was another reason I entrusted that responsibility to one person only. This late in life, after too many years of starting and stopping, I *knew* this book had to be birthed—now or never. And frankly, I was afraid that others would tell me that there were already enough books about women's careers or that I'd missed the mark, or that there were better things I should be doing with my time.

I know. For someone who writes about courage, I didn't have very much, at least when it came to book-writing. Thank you, Nancy, for telling me to keep going. You made me make it happen.

Still, there are many other people to thank. *Rise Like a Woman* is based on a program I developed and ran for twelve years in Australia, and I continue to run it in the US.

Confidentiality and space limitations mean that I can't list the women who were in the programs through the years, but you know who you are. And I want to say to each of you:

- I remember you. I remember your stories, your frustrations, and your successes.
- You matter. You grew. And it was thrilling to watch.
- Some of you will see your stories in this book (with names and details changed).

In addition, I'd like to express my gratitude and best wishes to every coaching client I've worked with (for too many years to count). Thank you for trusting me. Each one of you has your own permanent place in my heart.

I'd also like to call out other people who supported me with these and other programs.

Most recently in Saint Louis, I would like to thank Annie Schlafly, Susan Gobbo, and Suzanne Sierra for the opportunity to work with amazing, courageous international women.

Prior to that, I'd like to thank the Australian leaders who believed I had something to offer to *their* people: Rachel Slade, Susan Bannigan, Peter Hanlon, Amy Lyden, Ross Miller, Robyn Whittaker, Deanne Stewart, Maree Taylor, Peter Coleman, Matthew Rady, Phil Hay, and many more I haven't listed here.

To other wonderfully supportive colleagues and friends: Barbara Harrison, Tony Mathers, Kate Walker, Matt Perry, Tanja Perl, Heather Dawson, Natalie Isaacs, Gillian Taylor, Devon Scheef, Nancy Wagner, Barbara Gross, Tricia Hiemstra, and Cathy O'Neil, thank you for being there and for not rolling your eyes when I talked about the book I was going to write.

Thank you to Roger Walker, who watched me sweat and fret over this manuscript for hours on end—actually, for years on end. You never doubted me (or if you did, you never told me).

To my daughter Alexandra, who appears in the book without the anonymity afforded to others. You give me hope. And my son, Matthew, who is a fearless truth-teller. You keep me grounded.

And finally, to Raj Sisodia. You have been my role model, my advocate, my sponsor, and my friend. My association with you has brought so much joy and fulfillment. My gratitude forever.

ABOUT THE AUTHOR

AMY POWELL IS a mother of two, a hiker and backpacker, coach, and conscious business consultant. Always on the move, she has transitioned from Missouri to Arizona to California to Australia to Oregon and, finally, back to Missouri.

As an executive coach, Amy has helped over one thousand leaders navigate through organizations of between forty and forty thousand people. She works with them through every transition in their careers, from first-time managers to C-Suite roles. Her clients have included Nike, Lam Research, Met Life, Equifax, KPMG, Westpac Banking Corporation, Macquarie Bank, Norton Rose Fulbright, and Merck KGaA.

She developed the group coaching program Women on the Move (now Women on the Rise) and has run the program for fifteen years. That program is the basis for much of what is shared in this book.

A passionate supporter of international women in the region, Amy has partnered with International Mentoring Saint Louis (IM STL) to develop a two-part program called International Women on the Rise that supports women who are new to the US to find jobs and thrive in their careers.

If you would like to work with Amy Powell, or have her run a workshop in your organization, contact her at:

www.riselikeawoman.com
Email: amypowell@business-on-purpose.com
LinkedIn: linkedin.com/in/amypowellbusinessonpurpose